Social Selling Mastery for Entrepreneurs

Social Selling Mastery for Entrepreneurs

Everything that you ever wanted to know about Social Selling

Chris J Reed

LinkedIn: www.linkedin.com/in/b2bsocialmarketing

Author Website: www.chrisjreed.com

Website: www.blackmarketing.com

Email: chris@blackmarketing.com

Mobile/Whatsapp: (+65)9026 1966

Skype: BlackMarketingGlobal

WeChat: LinkedInMarketing

1st Edition 2018

First Published in 2018 for Chris J Reed by Evolve Global Publishing

PO Box 327 Stanhope Gardens NSW 2768 info@evolveglobalpublishing.com

www.evolveglobalpublishing.com

Book Layout: © 2018 Evolve Global Publishing

ISBN: (Paperback) 978-1-64370-189-9 (Ingram)

ISBN: (Hardcover) 978-1-64440-914-5 (Ingram)

ISBN-13: 978-1724993113 (Createspace)

ISBN-10: 1724993119 (Createspace)

ISBN: 9780463313800 (Smashwords)

ASIN: B07G76ZQVV (Amazon Kindle)

This book is available on Barnes & Noble, Kobo, Apple iBooks (digital), and Google Books (digital).

TRADEMARKS:

Table of Contents

About the Author

Chris J. Reed is the only CEO with a Mohawk! He is also the most recommended LinkedIn marketing entrepreneur on LinkedIn with over 650 LinkedIn recommendations.

Chris is the most controversial LinkedIn marketing entrepreneur and CEO in Singapore—appearing on the front page of local newspapers for the wrong and right reasons, saying what he thinks, and engaging happily on LinkedIn and in the marketing and business press. He has created a classic "Marmite" personal brand. Love him or hate him, he's making a mark! Mumbrella called Chris, "the most colourful marketing founder".

Chris is also a three-time #1 international bestselling author with his books *Personal Branding Mastery for Entrepreneurs and LinkedIn Mastery for Entrepreneurs*, the #1 book about LinkedIn on Amazon as well as this one *Social Selling Mastery for Entrepreneurs*. Chris's award-winning masterclasses are based on his best-selling *Mastery* books.

Chris has been named an Official LinkedIn Power Profile 2012–2018, has one of the world's most viewed LinkedIn profiles with 55,000 followers, and has won Social Media Entrepreneur of the Year Award and Asia's Most Influential Digital Media Professional Award by CMO Asia/World Brand Congress.

Chris is a serial, global entrepreneur, having created *Black Marketing—Enabling LinkedIn for You, The Dark Art of Marketing—*

Personal Branding for Entrepreneurs, Mohawk Marketing—TripAdvisor Engagement for You, Chris J. Reed Mastery—Masterclasses that Engage, Delight, Educate, and Entertain, and Spark: LinkedIn + Tinder = Match.

Black Marketing has just won Asia's Best Brand Award by CMO Asia and the Social Media Marketing Agency of the Year Award by Singapore Business Review.

Chris is also a vastly experienced LinkedIn and personal branding masterclass leader, event speaker, emcee, and chairperson. Chris lectures at the University of Hong Kong Business School, the Chinese University of Hong Kong Business School, and the National University of Singapore Business School to MBA students.

Chris also mentors for the CMO Council/Singapore Management University Business School and is chair of the marketing committee of the Singapore International Chamber of Commerce.

Introduction

From the three-time #1 bestselling author Chris J. Reed, "the only CEO with a Mohawk!" comes his latest book, *Social Selling Mastery for Entrepreneurs*. Whether you have heard the phrase "social selling" but don't know what it entails, or you have been trying to socially sell for years, this book will give you worthwhile insights, actionable advice, and secrets of the trade that Chris has learned in his ongoing career as a global social selling guru.

You see, Chris himself used social selling to create Black Marketing, the world's most recommended LinkedIn marketing agency, and Chris continues to rely on social selling for his business to thrive. Chris is the world's most recommended LinkedIn marketing masterclass instructor, entrepreneur and founder with 650 LinkedIn recommendations, triple LinkedIn marketing bestselling author, and the only entrepreneur or LinkedIn speaker on the site who is an Official LinkedIn Power Profile seven years running.

CEOs, entrepreneurs, and business leaders seek Chris out to gain support with their personal branding, social media presence, employer branding and social selling. In sharing his lessons learned and social selling dos and don'ts, *Social Selling Mastery for Entrepreneurs* offers an invaluable learning opportunity not to be passed up!

In *Social Selling Mastery for Entrepreneurs*, Chris explains how you, as a business owner and entrepreneur, a CEO, a CMO, or a sales or marketing professional can master social selling. Chris also lays out how LinkedIn, the only business-focused global social media platform, offers an ideal platform for social selling.

With LinkedIn's range of tools at your disposal for building your brand, releasing content, and connecting you with its 600 million-plus business professional users, Chris teaches you how to harness all

LinkedIn offers so that you can build your own social selling machine and keep it going at high speed for years to come.

In *Social Selling Mastery for Entrepreneurs*, you'll get a highly developed rendering of social selling, complete with anecdotes from Chris's career so that readers who aren't familiar with the concept can get on board fast. He then highlights the roles of social research, personal branding, and content marketing, showing how they work interdependently in social selling.

Additionally, Chris presents various content marketing strategies, as well as the nuances of content marketing you must consider to get the engagement you are aiming for. He presents a convincing case to get you writing and videoing yourself and putting that content out there because it's the people who show themselves to be thought leaders and experts that enjoy the greatest success in social selling.

As he often says in his highly recommended masterclasses, "Be more American and less English" on LinkedIn. What this means: be happy to promote yourself.

Authenticity, personalisation, recommendations, and even writing your own book are other critical elements in social selling that Chris details in this book so that you can develop yourself fully in the social selling arena.

Chris is upfront that LinkedIn is his preferred social media and social selling platform, and in *Social Selling Mastery for Entrepreneurs*, he shows you why it's such a potent platform. Also, he lays out how to use it fully. He starts with how to set up a convincing and impressive LinkedIn profile page and personal branding strategy. He explains how LinkedIn's publishing platform offers a fabulous medium for your content marketing. He goes into detail on using LinkedIn's premier, highly-refined search tool called Sales Navigator, so you can identify the most ideal prospective clients and buyers, and begin cultivating relationships with them.

He highlights how sending information via LinkedIn's PointDrive offers you valuable advantages and insights through the tracking data it delivers. Chris even shares the insights he's gathered from his experience engaging with his LinkedIn second and third connections to build new networks of supporters, potential clients, and actual clients in new cities where he's interested in doing new business all over the world.

In addition to his advice and insights, Chris also relates inspiring stories from his own career, about other LinkedIn users, and about today's incredible business giants. He cites Richard Branson, Ricco De Blank, Elon Musk, Arne Sorenson, and Candice Galek, so you can learn how they go about social selling and take cues from their success.

As Chris teaches in this book, social selling rests on building authentic relationships with individuals on social media and in real life. To do that, you need to harness all the tools that your social platform offers. People, relationships, content engagement, and the tools social media platforms offer are regularly changing. For this reason, you need to learn all you can to have the most options available for keeping up with the changes and building off your social selling successes.

Social Selling Mastery for Entrepreneurs offers a powerhouse education, so you can keep your social selling in top form and make adjustments big and small to stay in the game. Use this book to develop your social selling skillset, so you and your business can flourish, rather than flounder, in today's business reality of social selling.

Chapter 1
What Is Social Selling?

The Light Touch of Social Selling: Giving It Away

At its simplest, social selling is the process of developing one-on-one relationships as part of your selling method using social media to do so. Social selling is a very soft sell that rests on your ability to build authentic relationships with prospective customers through social media. By connecting and engaging together through social media about common business interests, you and your prospect build rapport. Over time, they gain trust in you, begin to value you as an expert, and seek out your products, services, or recommendations.

Because of social media, social selling is the most effective way of selling today. How it works is that in your social media platform—namely, LinkedIn, which I'll go into shortly—you openly share content that proves incredibly valuable to people interested in your area of business. Some of this content is not even connected to your business. Some of the content offers interesting angles as to why people may be interested in your business services. All of the content you offer will be entertaining and informative. In this way, you establish yourself as a trusted authority and at the same time build a strong personal brand.

Social selling is all about personalisation. Peer to peer. You to them. That is why we always advise people to write their LinkedIn profiles in the first person (i.e., I, me) not the third person (he, she, they, him, her, them). Imagine it's a networking event; you would never talk to anyone in the third person, so don't do that on LinkedIn.

Social selling is as much about getting someone to come to you as it is about you reaching out to them. But to do that, you must engage, enhance your LinkedIn profile, share curated and authentically created content, and give tips with no prospect of getting anything in return. You must also like, comment, and share other people's content that you genuinely think will be interesting to your followers. Engage, engage, engage.

Social selling is all about engaging. When someone else shares on LinkedIn, engage. People get notifications all the time on LinkedIn if someone likes, shares, or comments on a post. Not only are you genuinely engaging and sharing content with your followers from someone else, you're letting the person know that you shared it, that you're doing it for them. Socially selling is soft selling, not hard selling.

In liking, commenting, and sharing another person's content, you're reminding them that you have a business relationship so that if that person ever needs your services or is asked about your service, they are much more likely to remember your brand, your service, and what you do. Give, share. Don't just expect and sell; be social. Engage.

While 75% to 95% of people will put into action themselves the recommendations and ideas you give away, a good 5% to 25% will determine, "This is too much for me." Those are the ones who will contact you to buy your product or service. And even amongst the 75% to 95% that don't do actual business with you, they will still value you and what you do, so they'll be recommending you to their contacts and contacts of contacts, much of which will result in actual business for you down the road.

The point is that you attract clients to your business through social engagement with them, not by hard selling them at every opportunity.

Let me give an example of social selling that's light on social media, just so you get the idea. Say somebody comes to Asia and asks me, "Chris, can you introduce me to people? Can you help me with my LinkedIn profile?" I'll happily meet them for a cup of coffee and talk about how to do it. I'll give them one of my book. This is social selling in that I'm forming a relationship with them and establishing myself as a helpful expert to them; in the future, they might actually hire my company or recommend me to others.

Next time someone says to them, "Oh, your LinkedIn profile looks fantastic," they will respond, "Chris helped me out. He gave me a few tips, and I put them to action, so I could start a business." Later, these people might contact my company and engage our services. That's social selling in that it is indirect, soft, and entails a one-on-one relationship and it is centred around social media.

Strong Personal Brand

A lot of people get confused and think that leveraging their social media to sell a product or service is about selling a company. It's not about selling a company; it's about selling people, it's about selling you.

People buy people.

That's why building a strong personal brand is the key to successful social selling. If you think about the iconic brands of the world, like Richard Branson and Elon Musk, people are actually buying into them as individuals, and through that, they're buying into their services, brands, and products.

Because people have bought into his personal brand, Richard Branson can launch a hundred Virgin brands. Because people have bought into his personal brand, Elon Musk can sell flamethrowers, and Tesla and SpaceX can get away with losing money as investors have confidence in him. So, a huge part of social selling rests on the development of your own personal brand. It's something we'll go into more in this book.

The Optimal Platform

We've discussed two key elements of social selling—giving away valuable content and establishing a strong personal brand—now it's time to discuss the optimal platform for making all this happen: LinkedIn.

Because LinkedIn is almost the only social media platform that's available across the entire world that people can google, it's the go-to place for social selling. People can find you on LinkedIn through a Google search and from there, look at your profile, the content you are giving away, and read reviews and recommendations your clients post about working with you. They form a first impression of your personal brand through your LinkedIn profile.

They can actually contact those clients who have recommended you on LinkedIn to have a one-on-one conversation with them about you. In this way, LinkedIn allows you to establish yourself as a trusted expert and to build relationships with other people. And, it's these relationships which lead to sales.

LinkedIn offers tons of medium for you to use to share valuable and engaging content: Google Slides, Sales Navigator, PointDrive, PowerPoint, SlideShare, YouTube, Vimeo, etc.

Take PointDrive, for example. PointDrive is fantastic when it comes to social selling. You can share content, decks, white papers, videos, and products. On top of this, PointDrive allows you to track how people are responding to your content. It allows you to determine the impression people have of your personal brand on LinkedIn. You can track whether people are recommending you freely and openly on LinkedIn as well. PointDrive is such an impressive tool, you'll find a whole chapter dedicated to it later in this book!

LinkedIn is very much a social selling platform, a sales and marketing platform, and also a thought leadership platform. It is now the biggest publishing platform in the world. Anyone can write a blog, a short post, upload a video post, and create thought leadership, which enables them to be thought leaders and use content marketing to drive their social selling.

When I put content out there, I get someone to react to me on LinkedIn. I then follow up with a conversation. It's classic social selling. I am doing the reacting because they're doing the pushing, in effect. They have reacted to my content. They have reacted to my personal branding.

I also optimise my profile on LinkedIn through various hacks to create awareness and bring it to the public interest of my target audience. They then see what I do and come to my profile. I effectively SEO my LinkedIn profile to make the most searched for profile on LinkedIn. Organically and authentically.

People are already approaching me by viewing my profile and engaging with my content. Then I have a conversation with them. I often reach out to say thank you for viewing my profile, thank you for engaging, thank you for commenting, and start a conversation with them.

This is classic inbound social selling through an engaged social media strategy.

In this way, we are building a relationship that down the road might lead to actual sales or to one of us recommending the other to our contacts.

Social Research

Another great platform that demonstrates a singular aspect of social selling exceptionally well is TripAdvisor. You look at a hotel or restaurant on TripAdvisor, for example, before you actually buy the product, or in this case, book at the hotel or make a booking at the restaurant.

Your impression of the hotel or restaurant isn't about how it looks. It's about the positive or negative impression you get of it based on people's reviews of it and its overall rating on TripAdvisor.

You do your own research—social research—before you make a purchase. Buyers or clients doing social research about you is a key part of social selling, whether that research happens on TripAdvisor, LinkedIn, or Google.

You are actually selling yourself on LinkedIn, you're selling your company on LinkedIn, you're selling your brand on LinkedIn, you're selling your services on LinkedIn, and you're selling your employer branding on LinkedIn. And you're doing it very much through social selling because you're doing it through the impressions that people get from your photo, background picture, headline, summary, experience, recommendations, and the content that you're sharing.

Through all these, people are doing social research about you to determine their impression of you as a person. If the impression is positive, then they will make contact with you.

In this way, a relationship starts; a relationship that could very well lead to sales. This is how social research gets played out in social selling.

From Relationships to Sales

By helping people, either directly helping them if they message you on LinkedIn or less directly through some valuable content you share, people get a positive impression of your personal brand. Then they see what you do, what you're selling, and what your services are.

Next, they will find out more information about those particular services. In this way, you start a relationship with them. Social selling is all about relationships. It's all about building social media relationships so that people will buy from you.

Social selling is about building relationships and building them online, through social media, content, connections, shared connections, insights, and having discussions that are *not* anonymous.

On LinkedIn, you know exactly who people are. You both know each other's motives and ambitions, who they worked for, where they studied, who you both know. All the data is there. You can see where others are coming from, and you'll get insights from other people as a result.

You'll get insights from people that you never expected, and vice versa. You build relationships globally as a result of these connections, and you use other people's connections to actually leverage your social selling techniques (and vice versa). You help them. They help you. It's all the wonders of social selling on LinkedIn.

The New Reality of Sales

As we'll cover in chapters 2 and 3, the old ways of selling are dead. Cold-calling doesn't work. Neither does the individual or company web page. Social selling is the new avenue for business success.

If you haven't started social selling on LinkedIn, it's about time you do before your competitors do. For those still sceptical, the next chapter addresses this very issue: the reality of how buying is done in the current social media age.

Chapter 2

B2B Buying in the Age of Social Media

It is said that nearly all people have actually decided what product or service to buy before they've even encountered it. This also applies to B2B buying too. How is that?

People research, research, research, research in B2B as much as in B2C. People buy in the age of social media simply through research. Social media has allowed people to research more than ever before, and for B2B, this is often through LinkedIn.

They can research every single angle and aspect of a brand—from its customer service to its ethics, corporate social responsibility, community engagement, and treatment of employees or the environment. They can research the CEO personally—what the CEO is saying, wearing, eating, doing, and buying. Social media has allowed people to research everything, so they can make a decision before they even encounter a product or service.

How It Works

When people are deciding whether or not to buy from you, they research. The first thing that happens is they'll do a Google search about you. The results from this search: at the top of the page your LinkedIn profile comes up. It's among the first three results Google posts. When people click on your LinkedIn, they'll get a positive impression if you have a positive photograph, a positive background picture, a positive description, a positive summary, positive content, recommendations, and lots of positive engagement on your page as well.

Your content is positive and thought leading when it shows short form posts, long form posts, videos, graphs, grids, white papers, photographs, and figures that explain what you do, how you do it, and what you can do for people. When others are engaging with your content, it's an even greater sign that you know what you're doing and are an expert in this field.

Most importantly, when your content imparts genuinely helpful tips that people can put to use, that's when people viewing your LinkedIn will come to see you as an expert. A LinkedIn profile like this will make the people researching you think, "She really knows what she's doing."

From there, people researching you are going to look for reviews. They want to know what others are saying about you, what it's like to work with you, or what it's like to buy a product from you. On your LinkedIn page, you can post reviews from your clients and customers.

What's great about reviews and social media in this age of social selling is that in the end, people, businesses, and products that truly deliver end up getting rewarded. Think about it, you really can't gamify reviews. If a restaurant has gotten 500 reviews on TripAdvisor, and 300 of them are positive, then those good reviews outweigh the bad. When you read reviews, you'll see that people are reviewing every aspect of a business.

Take a restaurant featured on TripAdvisor; reviewers judge its food (of course), but also the experience, the general manager, the employees, the bathrooms, the music, the cutlery, the decor, and how the brand comes across on social media. In this way, social media goes across both business-to-business (B2B) and business-to-customer (B2C) realms.

Obviously, people research more on B2C, whether on Amazon or on TripAdvisor, but don't underestimate the power of research on B2B. People research my business, Black Marketing, all the time. They look at my videos on YouTube, my books, my blogs, my connections, and my reviews and recommendations.

People can actually read the real reviews and recommendations that my clients have written about me and my company Black Marketing from my LinkedIn profile. More importantly, they can click through to those clients (which is why we put it on LinkedIn as both a PointDrive and SlideShare deck as well as LinkedIn listing them on everyone's profiles, not on our website).

People can click through to those clients' profiles and talk to those people about what it was like to hire me and Black Marketing. They can write to previous clients to ask, "What was it like to work with Chris? What was his talk like? What was his masterclass like? What was he like in a one-on-one situation? What was he like as a leader? What was he like as a boss? What did Black Marketing do? How well did Black Marketing do?"

LinkedIn also allows people researching you to contact you and read your correspondences when you've been contacted by others. In this way, they can evaluate how engaging, responsive, and personable you are. I personally reply to all comments, likes, and shares that people post to me. I answer every single one because that's also key to how people research and buy. They judge, "How engaged is this person/brand? If I ask a question, how available and engaged is this person?" Your level of authentic engagement is important to people and something they look for when they research.

Every single person is checking you out and deciding whether to buy from you or work with you *before* they actually meet you, so don't think you can hide yourself away from social selling and social media. Don't think you can make your business work by falling back on old-school methods like cold-calling.

People are researching you, whether you like it or not!

The great thing about it is that you can take the bull by the horns and proactively craft your LinkedIn profile to guide their research on you. In this way, you are the one writing your narrative and deciding their opinion of you, a position you want to be in so that your social selling can take off!

In case you aren't convinced, the next chapter addresses the ineffectiveness of that old-school method of cold-calling. Also, we'll address why email mass marketing and unsolicited group chats on WhatsApp and beyond don't work either. Yes, indeed, it's all about one-on-one authentic relationship building, that is, if you want to sell . . .

Chapter 3

Cold-Calling Is Dead: Why You Must Start Social Selling

In the age of social media, cold-calling simply does not work.

Making unsolicited calls to people to get them interested in a product or service is not effective these days. It just doesn't work that way anymore. Times have changed, so you better change with them.

Cold, Unknown, Unsolicited = Ineffective

I live in Singapore and get many independent financial advisers and estate agents cold-calling me from India, Singapore, and even the USA. I know from experience that every time I answer an unknown phone number, it's going to be someone I don't want to talk to. Therefore, I no longer pick up these kinds of calls.

I know many CEOs and CMOs who do the same. They will not answer their phones when they see an unknown number because they figure that it's a cold-caller. Consequently, cold-calling is dead. But that's not all . . .

Email marketing is also completely dead in my view. Spam filters and the EU's General Data Protection Regulation (GDPR) have contributed to the futility of email marketing. Even more than that, trends show that people simply don't want to waste their precious time (or risk dealing with a virus or scam) opening an unsolicited email from a person or business that they don't recognise.

To take it even farther, when people add me to unsolicited WhatsApp or WeChat groups and so forth, I leave immediately. Why? It's the same as cold-calling and email marketing—if I don't know a particular person, who they are and why I should engage with them, then I don't want to waste my time bothering.

I need to know who someone is first and have some confidence about their personal branding, what they're selling, whether I'm interested, and why they're engaging with me, for me to take the time and energy to have some kind of group conversation with them. And I'm no anomaly in feeling this way. Cold-calling, whether via phone, email, or another medium, no longer works.

So, what does work?

How can we engage with new people to eventually win their business? You should already know how I'm going to answer. It's what this book is about: social selling. More specifically, social selling through LinkedIn.

Social Selling on LinkedIn = Warm and Inviting

The reason cold-calling doesn't work is that it's cold. People don't know who you are, what you stand for, who you are connected to, and how you can really help them. Socially selling, particularly on LinkedIn, answers all these questions, which sets the groundwork for a genuine relationship to build in which both parties can benefit.

If you set up a great LinkedIn profile and you've enhanced your personal brand, when you message a new person over LinkedIn, they can go to your profile and see exactly who you are and who vouches for you—in one step. LinkedIn has no spam box, so you don't have to worry about your message getting sent to a spam box.

For example, you could send a brief message, saying, "Because your LinkedIn profile shows you're in the business of Y, I'd like to talk to you about how we could work together. Look at my profile, my content, and my company to learn more about me. Also, notice from my connections that we both know X. Send me a message, so we can set up a time to talk."

Whether it ends up being a sales conversation or a relationship-building conversation where they recommend you and you recommend them, both are great. Social selling is about meeting people in real life or on Skype, Zoom, WeChat, or Whatsapp. Once both parties recognize that both have professional brands and goals and connections in common, something that LinkedIn facilitates, then a relationship can start from there.

Social selling is not about locking in a sale on the first contact. Social selling is much more about giving people information, building relationships, and then seeing how it works when it comes to personal chemistry later on when you meet or have a phone call.

In social selling, the first thing that happens is establishing rapport, empathy, and shared interests and goals. All that has to happen before any selling occurs.

Six Reasons Social Selling Is In and Cold-Calling Is Out

Here are the six main reasons that social selling has replaced cold-calling as the way to sell a product or service. Consider this a chapter review.

Reason 1—*Cold-calls are not given the time of day. They are easily identified and dismissed.*

The only calls I get nowadays that I don't recognise are from cold-callers. I typically ignore them. On the odd occasion, I accidentally answer the call, I instantly regret it, particularly when it's either a wealth management salesperson or a bank.

I hang up quickly. Unsurprisingly, I am not alone. According to Harvard Business Review, 90% of C-suite executives say they never respond to cold-calls. I think this applies to unsolicited emails and group chats as well.

Reason 2—*LinkedIn offers the optimal space for connecting with others to do business with.*

There are over 600 million professionals on LinkedIn. Basically, you can reach anyone who is anyone on LinkedIn, either directly through InMails and groups, or indirectly through a connection, whether that is a first, second, or third connection.

This is even more apparent in countries with particularly high LinkedIn penetration rates, like the US, UK, Canada, Australia, Singapore, Hong Kong, and New Zealand, plus countries with the highest world populations, like China, India and Brazil. Penetration rates are high for many European countries too.

Because everyone on LinkedIn has a profile, it allows people to do extensive research on anyone that reaches out to them. This means messages from new people are "warm," as opposed to out-of-the-blue and suspicious like a cold-call. As we know personally, we respond to warmth.

When we can quickly and easily learn about a new person from perusing their profile—their background, interests, associates, and even their face—then we are more inclined to engage with them. That's why LinkedIn is such a valuable platform for social selling.

Reason 3—*Of all salespeople, 78% of those using social media, like LinkedIn, outsell their peers.*

You are almost five times more likely to schedule the first meeting with a new person if you have a personal LinkedIn connection with them.

Reason 4—*LinkedIn enables you to learn everything you need to about the person that wants to do business with you or that you want to do business with.*

In this way, LinkedIn is an optimal platform for people doing research and connecting with others whom they might want to do business with. Once you receive a message from a person on LinkedIn, you can check out exactly who they are and whether you wish to do business with them (this is "social research"). You can look at the following:

- Their profile (If they have no photo, then they are a no. If they have less than one hundred connections, then they are a no.)
- Their connections (Are they connected to people you know? Can you ask your connections about them?)
- Their company page (No company page, then they are a no.)
- Their content marketing strategy (No blog or no recent updates, then they're a no.)

Then and only then, you will find an answer to whether you feel that the person or company is one that you wish to be doing business with (and vice versa).

Reason 5—*A majority of decision-makers are using LinkedIn to make purchasing decisions.*

Seventy-five percent of business-to-business buyers and 84% of C-level and vice president (VP) executives surveyed by the International Data Corporation (IDC) use social media to make purchasing decisions. Of these, 56% have decided to buy before they even meet the contact.

In other words, before they even meet you, they have already decided whether to do business with you. The rest is down to you, the quality of your LinkedIn page, your reviews and recommendations, and the rapport you build. It's also down to price. The rest is done.

Reason 6—*Social buying correlates with buying influence, according to the IDC survey.*

The average business-to-business buyer who uses social media for buying support is more senior, has a bigger budget, makes more frequent purchases, and has a greater span of buying control than a buyer who does not use social media. Because we all want to be doing business with such big players, you gotta have a great LinkedIn presence to be in contention. Cold-calling sure won't get you anywhere with them.

Every single person is checking you out, doing social research on you, and deciding whether to buy from you or work with you *before* they actually meet you, so don't think you can hide yourself away from social selling and social media.

Don't think you can make your business work by falling back on old-school methods like cold-calling. People are researching you, whether you like it or not! The great thing about it is that you can take advantage of this new reality and proactively craft your LinkedIn profile to make social selling work in your favour!

This is also one of the reasons that I tell people not to scrape the data off LinkedIn and email people. What happens if you do this?

Firstly, it goes to someone's spam box or promotions box. I receive thousands of emails a day that I never see because I use Google's five folders to manager my email, and the system knows when something is a promotion or an update, and not a genuine message from a genuine person. They can also tell if it's sent from MailChimp or some other platform. It immediately goes into one of the folders I never check consistently, not to my primary one that I check multiple times each day.

The other reason not to scrape info from LinkedIn is a legal one. You're currently breaking the law if this person is in the EU, and many other countries also have similar data privacy laws.

The main reason though: why would you? You spent all that time and resources on developing your personal brand on LinkedIn and a content marketing strategy on LinkedIn, and then you want to move that target to a platform where they will 1) never see your email and 2) never see who you are, what your personal brand stands for, your content strategy, who you both know, your recommendations . . . why would you want to do that?

Ultimately, social selling is about getting social with people, that means engaging together. In the next chapter, we'll review some ways to make yourself more inviting, so others will clamour to engage with you—and eventually buy from you.

Chapter 4

People Buy People: Social Selling Is Just That, Social

A fundamental rule about social selling is to remember that people buy people. Social selling rests on you getting social with the people you reach out to. What does it mean to be social in this context? It means a few things. That's what we'll cover here.

Sharing Really Is Caring

When "people buy people," that entails one person evaluating another person (i.e., doing social research) to determine whether they buy into their credibility, reputation, delivery, results, and reviews and recommendations from previous clients.

For example, when people are deciding whether to buy from me and Black Marketing, they are going to look at my LinkedIn profile, my books, my thought leadership, my videos, and my talks. They are going to look at other people's reviews of me and my work, and their reports about the levels of success I helped them reach. All of these things factor into my credibility, responsibility, reputation, delivery, and results; consequently, they all influence whether or not people will "buy" me.

To aid people when they are researching me to decide if I'm the person they want to "buy," so to speak, I share all my talks on YouTube. I'm not concerned that people can copy all my tips and go away and do it themselves rather than hire Black Marketing. I actually love that. I was in Hong Kong last week, and I did three talks. I videoed them all, and they're all going on LinkedIn or YouTube. So I'm sharing, sharing, sharing, sharing.

I don't believe that there's any intellectual property in my talks that anybody else can't figure out for themselves. I'm just making it easy for people by sharing these talks and looking at good business karma. I share on the basis that people will put my advice about social selling and branding into action and then credit me and Black Marketing for helping them socially sell their business, build their reputation, and build their brand, all of which will add to my own and Black Marketing's increased credibility and positive reputation.

As a result, when other people are looking to buy the kind of services Black Marketing offers, they will encounter lots of folks crediting me and Black Marketing for the great work we do. As I said, people are looking to buy people.

The takeaway here: because people buy people, your reputation means a lot. A way to increase your reputation is to share valuable content with everyone.

Personalisation

When someone reaches out to you or you reach out to someone else—because people buy people—it's important to make your correspondence personal. Show that you know something about them in particular, whether it's something you gathered from their profile page, from an event that you both attended, or from a concept, product, or business philosophy you both appreciate.

For example, consider: are you both entrepreneurs? Are you CEOs in Singapore or Stockholm or Mexico City? Are you expats? Are you both expats/immigrants? Did you both get MBAs in London? What do you have in common? You figure this out and relate it in your message because being personal is key in social selling. Why? Because people buy people.

This is what I do. Say, I meet someone at a talk, networking event, chamber event, or masterclass. Both before the event, if I know they're coming and later after the event, I make a point of connecting with them by sending them a personalised message. I might say how I am looking forward to meeting them or thank them for coming to the masterclass.

When I do this, I always get people coming up to me at these events and saying hi, thanks for connecting on LinkedIn, and we start a conversation. They will obviously know me and recognise me because of my Mohawk, but they also really appreciate that I bothered to reach out before the event. It's also very likely that I was the only person to have actually done this.

If people engage or reply to my messages on LinkedIn, whether they decline or accept my InMails, I'll write a follow-up message saying, "It would be great to connect with you, regardless of whether you want to do business or not. We're in the same space, so it would be great to share content." In this way, I'm making my contact with them personal and genuine.

You see, I really mean it when I say, "regardless of whether or not you want to do business," because I've learned so much and gotten so much value from so many people whom I connected with but haven't actually done business with. How? That brings us to the next point . . .

Recommendations

Because I've got 10,000+ first connections on LinkedIn in Singapore alone, I can target two million people in Singapore (of its LinkedIn population of 2.3 million) in my first, second, third, and group connections. Wow—that's some serious reach! People are buying people. It's all about the "three degrees of separation".

How this plays out is, say, a person named Lina is looking for help with branding her business. Lina then asks her group for any recommendations. Someone in her group might be directly connected with me and Black Marketing, or they might know another person who is connected with me—these are those first, second, third, and group connections at play.

The point is that even if most of my 10,000 positive first connections haven't done actual business with me, we are connected and they are at the ready to recommend me to someone like Lina looking for the kind of services Black Marketing offers. This is social selling and people buying people.

When someone in Lina's circle recommends me and Black Marketing to her, Lina can then go to my LinkedIn profile and peruse it to find clients that I've worked with. She can contact them to talk about what it was like working with me and get their genuine impressions.

The takeaway: recommendations go a long way in social selling. These can be recommendations from clients you've actually worked with, or they might be recommendations from second, third, or group connections who enjoy engaging with you over shared content. Recommendations are so important that you'll find a whole chapter dedicated to them later in the book.

The Ice-Breaker Advantage

Since people are buying people, it's all about being social. I believe that LinkedIn is a catalyst to meet people, whether it's on Zoom, Skype, or in real life. I love to go to Hong Kong, Shanghai, or Sydney, and meet real people in real life at real events. I enjoy seeing them do talks, sharing information, sharing engagements, and then seeing if we can do business together.

For me, a key to making these real-people meet-ups happen is that I offer a very recognisable ice-breaker: the Mohawk. Let me explain: last week I attended an American Chamber of Commerce event in Hong Kong with the chief executive of Hong Kong and various highfalutin people.

I was the only one there in black ripped jeans, a black rock t-shirt, black Dr. Martens, and a Mohawk. When I arrived, there were about ten people there who approached me and introduced themselves, saying, "Hey, we're connected on LinkedIn. We've never met before. It's fantastic to meet you."

I wouldn't have been able to do the same thing the other way around because I wouldn't know them from Adam. But they could do it for me because of the Mohawk. With my Mohawk, jeans, and t-shirt look, I stand out. Also, there were people there whom I did know from previous events, so I was able to say to them, "Don't we know each other? It's fantastic to reconnect."

The takeaway: social selling, even with great internet platforms like LinkedIn, is all about people buying people, which means people getting social and connecting face-to-face, whether at a conference, over coffee, or over a video call. A great way to achieve these real-life connections, especially at big events, is to stand out, to offer an ice-breaker, so people will recognise you. For me, it's the Mohawk. It allows me a quick way to get social and further my social selling.

What ice-breaker resonates with you? It's something to seriously consider because it will more readily facilitate others recognising you and engaging with you, which is what social selling is all about.

Just as an ice-breaker helps you stand out, it also serves to promote your personal brand. Chapter 5, which is up next, goes into personal branding and how it works in conjunction with social selling.

Personal Branding: Integral to Social Selling

Social selling is all about relationship-building and people buying people. It involves offering helpful content and contributing to conversations, which positions you as a personable expert, someone others want to do business with. It could be that others just like and comment on your contributions, and their connections see your content too.

As I've already explained, this is valuable because it builds your credibility and reputation so that first, second, third, and group connections will think of you when someone they know, who may not be connected to you, needs a recommendation.

Through this social aspect of social selling, your connections introduce you to some of the people they know. That's what I mean about social selling being social. It's all about using the social skills you have and the networking process on LinkedIn, as well as contributing valuable content to others through videos, books, articles, blogs, and commentary. In this way, you make more and more connections, and extend the reach of your reputation and credibility.

When you add in personal branding, the success of your social selling only grows. First, let's review what personal branding is. Then we'll explore how personal branding optimises social selling.

Personal Branding

Your personal brand is what people immediately think of when they hear your name. What are the value and adjectives associated with it? You are a brand just like Coke or Nike is, and they have values just like you have values.

Whether or not you actively guide and cultivate your brand, you still have one. If you aren't in charge of it, that means others are defining it for you. Personal branding, then, is how you establish, communicate, and promote yourself.

Personal branding is also your actions. People often have a perception of me before they meet or see me on stage that is different to when I deliver a blistering LinkedIn masterclass or demonstrate insights that can change and revolutionise their marketing and sales.

Personal branding is how you package and market yourself. When you have a well-established personal brand, it makes others more interested in engaging with you. Consequently, personal branding and social selling go hand-in-hand.

At Black Marketing, when we help people establish compelling personal brands, we recommend they concentrate on clearly defining their values, style, thought leadership, and platform, and that they start engaging in every way.

Values—at the heart of personal branding are your and your business's core values. What is important to you? What is important to your business? What do you stand for and not stand for? Don't make your values a mystery. Be very clear about your core values.

Style—remember in the previous chapter when I talked about ice-breakers? When you have a distinct style, something that stands out, for example, a Mohawk, a beard, a moustache, the way you dress, the way you look, or what you say—then people will remember you. You'll make a stronger and more certain impression.

Thought leadership—be provocative, be interesting, be controversial, but never be boring. When you offer genuine and interesting ideas, observations, and comments to your audience, you establish yourself as an expert and a leader.

Your platform—it could be LinkedIn, it could be YouTube, it could be Instagram, but ensure you choose a platform to communicate your personal brand.

My second book, *Personal Branding Mastery for Entrepreneurs,* goes into much more detail about personal brand and your personal branding strategy, and gives some great examples from the Joker to *Breaking Bad,* Darth Vader, and the Gladiator.

Brand CJR

I write all the time about my personal brand as I believe in practising what I preach. Personal branding needs to be authentic, and I am completely authentic in how I look and what I say. I am lucky because I am an entrepreneur and can do and say what I want. I have no bosses, and clients choose me or don't choose me, based on my very authentic personal branding.

In terms of my style, the visual element of it, there's the ever-changing coloured Mohawk, the colour black, my ripped black jeans, and black rock t-shirts along with black Doc Marten boots. People know who I am wherever I go. It's the perfect way to start a conversation.

Mumbrella called me the "most colourful marketing founder", and I have what many people consider to be a "Marmite" brand. You either love me or you hate me. I love that I split the room. That desire to provoke and generate thoughts in one direction or the other is an essential part of my personal branding.

I say what I think and am happy to inspire and annoy in equal measures. Engagement is based on passionate views and sharing your thoughts. "Be yourself", "Express yourself", and "Be true to yourself", are truisms that I live and die by.

As far as my thought leadership goes, I have strong ideas, views, and thoughts all of which I am always sharing over videos, articles, blogs, and books, and on other people's content. And my go-to platform, obviously, is LinkedIn.

To further help you understand personal branding, let me give you two people who function as brands: Richard Branson and Candice Galek. Richard Branson has 15 million followers on LinkedIn. He has nailed it to a T. Look at his pictures; look at his thought leadership. It's amazing.

Then there's Candice Galek. She is the number one profile on LinkedIn. Even though she only has 80,000 followers compared with Richard Branson's 15 million, she has been marketing herself and marketing Bikini Luxe through her thought leadership and her personal brand. She has generated an enormous amount of money, and she has a great content marketing strategy in terms of driving people to Bikiniluxe. com through personal branding and through thought leadership on LinkedIn.

Personal Branding and Social Selling

Social selling is about getting social and personal, about people buying people. For people to be interested in starting a relationship with you, they must see you as a whole person and know what you stand for (your values). They must literally see you and what they see should be distinct and personable (your style). They must know your perspectives and ideas on relevant issues (your thought leadership). They must be able to access you (your platform).

Therefore, the more developed your personal brand—your values, style, thought leadership, and platform—then the more of a whole person you'll come across to others, which certainly optimises your potential for getting social and building relationships, the foundation of social selling. Personal branding makes your "personhood" shine. It makes it pop. This puts you in a prime position for social selling, both on LinkedIn and beyond. That's why it's so important you put in the time and effort to craft your personal brand.

Creating Your Own Personal Brand

Look at your brand values and analyse yourself, just as you would another brand. Whether it is H&M, Moet and Chandon, or Newcastle United Football Club, regardless, it's a brand. So, look at your own values, just like you look at the brand values of Apple or Adidas. Identify your brand values, and then disseminate and promote those brand values.

For English and Asian readers: lots of English people and lots of Asian people want to be modest, which can go counter to personal branding. They don't want to tell people about themselves. They think it is over-promoting and over-publicising, but it is actually the only way that people find out about you.

While I recommend, "Be less English and be more American," really it's about going somewhere in between: don't be too American, but don't be too English. Go somewhere in the middle and talk about your achievements, and people will relate to that. People like success. In Asia, in particular, people like success.

LinkedIn is the platform I recommend for promoting your personal brand because it's the number one platform by far from a professional point of view. There are 600 million business people using LinkedIn, and these people are all engaging with each other on it on a professional basis.

You have the same amount of space on LinkedIn as Richard Branson and Candice Galek. You can be the next Candice Galek because you can promote yourself on LinkedIn better than anywhere else in the world in a professional context. That's why LinkedIn beats Facebook, Twitter, or Instagram, which are not professional. LinkedIn is professional and you're professional, so be on LinkedIn.

Everyone can see who you are, who you both know, where you work, and what you do on LinkedIn. People think twice before abusing someone else on LinkedIn. You can't be anonymous or fake like you can on Facebook or Twitter.

This also means that I can see everyone who comments, shares, and likes. I can determine who they are, who they work with or for, and whom we both know (our connections)—and they can do the same with me. You can't do that on the other platforms.

Your LinkedIn profile, including your picture, your strap-line, and your summary, are crucial in terms of promoting your personal brand. Your picture is your unique selling point. For me, it shows my Mohawk. Next is your strap-line. It's got to create an awareness of what you actually do.

At the moment my strap-line is that I am "the only CEO with a Mohawk". I also now use "the most recommended LinkedIn masterclass leader/entrepreneur".

Then, you have to look at your summary section. Your summary section describes you as a person. It's your brand values. Put in things there that are interesting and that are not just about your company, but your journey. What have you done? What are your successes? What have you learnt and what are you actually adding to communities? Why should people look at you? Why should people talk to you?

Social selling is about building relationships with people that may later result in sales. The more of a complete and capable person you can come across, the more others will want to engage in a relationship with you.

Because personal branding helps show you as a complete and adept person, it's key to social selling. Leverage all the tools LinkedIn offers to promote your personal brand, so you can optimise your social selling potential on the platform used by the most professionals worldwide.

In the next chapter, we'll compare LinkedIn and Facebook, so you can see why LinkedIn is the best option for business-to-business social selling.

Chapter 6

LinkedIn: The Hub of B2B Social Selling

There appears to be a very ill-informed debate about whether LinkedIn or Facebook is better for business-to-business (B2B) social selling. To me, it's a no-brainer: LinkedIn wins every time. Why bother wasting time on Facebook when Facebook simply won't work for you? Here are five reasons LinkedIn beats Facebook for business-to-business social selling.

1. Targeting, Sales Navigator, Data, and InMails

LinkedIn offers you an incredible breadth of data and very narrow, refined search options, which is fantastic. You can create any number of campaigns around content and advertising to target decision-makers in a warm and personal way. The ace in the pack, though, is Sales Navigator (more about that later in the book) and its data combined with InMails, invitation messages, and open profile messaging. With InMails, invitation messages, and open profile messaging you can target decision-makers with a warm, soft-selling mail that goes directly to their inbox.

To create your target list on LinkedIn, you can specify any criteria you want—company size, country, years of experience, groups joined, and position in the company and industry (among others)—to ensure that your InMail, first degree message, or open profile message (which you can only see on Sales Navigator) reaches the right person. You simply can't do this on Facebook. Because social selling is about people buying people, making sure your message reaches the right person is key.

2. Warm Leads and Personal Branding

There are no cold leads on LinkedIn. Why do LinkedIn's InMails work? Why does content marketing on LinkedIn work? The person sending the InMail can check your personal profile on LinkedIn to learn about you, which is why personal branding is so important. The person receiving your InMail can check out your personal profile, your company profile, any mutual connections you both share, and the content that you have shared. This ability to research you makes you more inviting to them. It adds warmth to your InMail. None of this can be done in a business context on Facebook.

For this very reason, personal branding in a business context has never been more important than on LinkedIn. If you have an incomplete personal or company profile, and you don't share interesting content, then your InMails and social selling attempts will more than likely fail.

On LinkedIn, you can also contact people who have viewed your profile, who have engaged with you on a business discussion within a group, who have shared your business content, who are second or third degree connections, or who have been recommended by your contacts on LinkedIn. All of this enhances your understanding of who they are to you and who you are to them, so that if you reach out to them, you have deeper insights to build a relationship off of.

Since you have checked out their business profile on LinkedIn, and because you have already shared business content and started to build a business relationship, you are essentially creating a warm lead towards building a potentially beneficial relationship, which is what social selling is all about. This is so much better than cold-calling, cold emailing, or cold contacting via Facebook.

3. Context

Facebook is a social, personal platform. LinkedIn is a business platform. It's worth reiterating this fact because there are people on both platforms who use each application as if it were the other. If you're a CEO of a large company or an SME, and you have a personal Facebook account that is filled with personal content about family and friends, do you really want to be contacted by someone who is selling you services while you have your family/personal hat on? The answer is likely no.

LinkedIn is a business platform. When you are contacted on LinkedIn, it is for business reasons, in a business context, and not a purely social or personal one. If you contact this same CEO on LinkedIn, they will look at your message in a business context; conversely, they would likely ignore it or be annoyed by the same approach on Facebook. On LinkedIn, they will have their business hat on. It's all about the context of your approach and the platform you choose for social selling to work. The fact is, people tend to keep very different and separate profiles (or "hats") for these two different platforms. Respect this and you will benefit.

4. Content Marketing

Content engagement is a cornerstone of social selling, a topic we'll be going into in detail in this book. You can create a business-focused content marketing plan on LinkedIn. Since LinkedIn is based entirely on a proactive content marketing strategy, it will enable you to engage potential customers as well as win new business via content engagement. Potential clients and partners can get to know you and what you do through your content. It's a very warm and effective way to generate reactive business lead generation and to succeed with proactive business proposals.

People buy people. They are much more likely to accept your InMail or connection request if they have heard of you and/or read your content; if they think both are interesting and relevant to their business; and if they are under the impression that you know what you are talking about.

You can't do this kind of social selling on Facebook because it's not a business platform.

5. Company Pages

There is a world of difference between a company page on LinkedIn and one on Facebook.

Business-to-customer (B2C) brands thrive on Facebook. Brands on Facebook will even admit that it's very hard to prove that any of the "likes" can be connected directly to sales. Coca-Cola's chief marketing officer famously confirmed this sentiment last year in regards to their 60 million Facebook fans when he reported that he couldn't track any sales to any of these millions of likes.

So there you have it: LinkedIn beats Facebook for business-to-business social selling. These five reasons are striking, and you can look to the success Black Marketing is enjoying if you want a sixth reason to go with LinkedIn over Facebook for B2B social selling.

You can also leverage LinkedIn to socially sell to high net worth individuals, like the C-suite executives whom you are engaging within B2B social selling. In the next chapter, you'll learn how LinkedIn is the optimal platform for social selling in the B2C space when the C is high net worth customers.

Chapter 7

LinkedIn: Elemental in B2C Social Selling with Affluent Customers

At the same time that you are using LinkedIn to do amazing B2B social selling, you are developing relationships not only with other businesses but also with particular high net individuals in those businesses. Consequently, as you are developing relationships that could lead to B2B sales, these relationships could also lead to B2C sales, when those high net individuals get personally interested in and impressed by your products or services. Social selling on LinkedIn can be a powerful twofer. Let me lay it out with an example.

A Conference and an Anniversary Celebration? Perfect!

Take a five-star hotel like the Ritz-Carlton in Hong Kong.

Over LinkedIn, this hotel establishes relationships with C-level executives in numerous businesses. Some, perhaps many, of these relationships will lead to sales on both the B2B and B2C levels for the five-star hotel. For instance, say a business decides to hold a conference at the Ritz-Carlton in Hong Kong. The Ritz-Carlton knows very well that although this is a B2B sale, high net individuals attending the conference will be spending time in the hotel with their C-suites and teams. Consequently, all of these attendees are potential B2C sales.

Just imagine a CEO at the conference in the Ritz-Carlton in Hong Kong thinking to themselves, "Wow. This space is fantastic. Maybe I could have my daughter's 21st birthday here? I'd love to have my 50th birthday here." The point is that what brought the CEO to the Ritz-Carlton was a B2B experience—but that could very well lead to a B2C sale as well.

LinkedIn, the Golden Ticket

LinkedIn's special data offerings and refined search powers make it the best platform for achieving these B2C social sales, even when B2B is your primary concentration. Here's another example to show what I mean.

At Black Marketing we work with several financial services firms, for example, where we beef up their personal branding. Of course, we are aiding them in their B2B selling, but at the same time, we keep in mind B2C sales that could result as well. What we do is use LinkedIn's particular data offerings and its Sales Navigator to narrow our search and target affluent expats in Singapore and Hong Kong, for example. So we're using a B2B platform to target B2C.

We can identify exactly who's a CEO and who's an expat using the data and targeted search options on LinkedIn. After building a strong personal brand for the financial adviser, complete with white papers, videos, recommendations, and more to show that the financial adviser is an expert, we can then start building a relationship—social selling—with the targeted CEOs, affluent expats, etc., whom LinkedIn allows us to identify.

Using LinkedIn's Sales Navigator, we can identify high net individuals and reach out to them on LinkedIn to actually sell to them. In this way, we can achieve both B2B and B2C sales using LinkedIn. For high net worth individuals, LinkedIn is key.

When it comes to events, as well, you can have conferences and events, which can be B2B or B2C. LinkedIn's phenomenal for that because you can sell directly to customers using infographics, videos, and information codes without your content or messages getting allocated to spam.

Black Marketing is hosting a conference in a few months. To attract attendees, we're using Sales Navigator, inputting a special code to reach people in Singapore who are in sales and marketing as well as CEOs. Once we identify them, we begin the social selling, offering them videos and articles that provide valuable advice and at the same time create awareness about Black Marketing. In this way we are building relationships both on the B2B and B2C levels in hopes of making sales on these same levels too. LinkedIn offers us—and everyone—a powerful B2B and B2C social selling platform.

To attract people to your brand and maintain their attention, you must offer them something. That's what the next chapter addresses: your content marketing strategy.

Chapter 8

Content Marketing: The Heart of Social Selling

Because social selling is about building relationships, those relationships must be built off of something. They must have something at their foundation that encourages engagement. And what is that?

Content.

Content that informs, provokes, reveals, challenges, suggests, questions, and educates others so that they and their businesses can perform better.

In order to provoke engagement and interaction—which is what social selling is all about—you must be intentional about how you handle content. You must be intentional about your content marketing strategy.

In determining your particular approach to content marketing, there are a number of factors to consider. The primary factor: you have to think about what your clients are interested in. You have to think about their interests as well as the interests of your peers, stakeholders, managing directors, CEOs, and employees.

If you employ people, what do your employees think about particular kinds of content? If you have shareholders, what are their concerns and interests? How do you instigate and inspire confidence? Think about every single thing you share, comment on, and like because that all adds up—positively or potentially negatively—to you as a personal brand and as a company brand.

What's your content marketing strategy? If you don't have one, then you still have one—it's just a flat zero in marketing strategy. You are very much using (or should use) content marketing to elevate your personal brand and company brand on LinkedIn.

Six Options for Your LinkedIn Content Marketing

Content marketing is all about how you market your personal brand and company brand on LinkedIn. There are essentially six different ways to do content marketing on LinkedIn.

1: Focus on the content of others

The first and most obvious strategy is to concentrate on other people's content and like it, share it, and comment on it. That way you're taking part in a conversation because—remember—social selling is all about getting social. By involving yourself in others' content, you're letting people know who you are and where you stand.

For example, by using LinkedIn's Sales Navigator you can closely identify and target promising leads. Once you've done that, you can focus on their content, commenting on it, sharing it, and liking it. In doing so, a notification will pop up both in their LinkedIn and email to say that you have commented, liked, or shared their content. In this way, these potential leads get your name.

Over time with your regular engagement with their content, they'll investigate your profile and will likely get a favourable impression of what you do. They'll think, "That's fantastic. Adriana shared this, Adriana liked this, or Adriana commented on this. Absolutely fantastic." They'll start paying attention to you and start engaging with you.

In this way, a relationship begins to build.

2: Curate content from outside sources

This second content marketing strategy involves sharing relevant and provocative content from outside sources; that is, content you've found but not created yourself. This is a curated content strategy. You can do this by looking for information anywhere. It could be from *The Guardian*, from *Marketing Magazine,* or from the *Financial Times.*

In this strategy, you pick content you think is relevant to your target audience of peers, clients, and others whom you'd like to engage with, and you share that content. It's important that you are sharing content that's valuable and interesting in a business context. From here, the relationship building—and social selling—increases. These people will then engage with each other and with you around that interesting content, which puts you and your business on their radar, which can lead to sales down the road.

3: Post photographs in a business context

As simple as it sounds and as easy as it is to do, posting original photographs on LinkedIn is an effective content marketing strategy. People like seeing photographs on LinkedIn because it's your original content, and it's you being personal and doing something in a business context.

And remember—people buy people. Photographs show you as a person. When you post photographs that depict other people in them, and those people see their image on your page, it makes them feel seen and valued. It provokes them to start engaging with you, which is how a relationship builds and social selling gets activated.

Whenever I give a talk, I take a photograph of people there at the venue. Later, I post the photograph on my LinkedIn profile, write a relevant caption, and also tag the people in the photograph. Then I find these people on LinkedIn to share it with them. When I meet interesting people, fellow authors, and fellow entrepreneurs, I get photos and share and tag them as well. Doing this jump-starts relationship and social selling.

4: Specialise in infographics

Infographics—charts or diagrams that visually represent data or information—are an amazing and effective way to communicate interesting content on LinkedIn. You can find intriguing infographics and share those, or you can make your own infographics. For example, it's not difficult to take a few basic digest reports and transform them into an infographic.

In addition to sharing infographics, you can share the report you got your information from, which then will drive people back to where that report is, whether that's on a LinkedIn profile, SlideShare, or an actual website. It's very much about using LinkedIn to leverage what you want to tell people using infographics.

Infographics can also be simple things like screen grabs or even things around different parts of your particular brand. You can use infographics as a way of challenging a perception of your brand. You can communicate, "Well, actually, my brand is this, *not* this", or "It's this *and* this".

Infographics are a great way of sharing content and engaging people. People like infographics because they're both personal and also about business. Plus, infographics are content that people can share.

5: Be a thought leader. Create your own content

Probably the hardest thing to do on LinkedIn is creating original content. It takes time and effort, but it's what can make you a thought leader. You come up with an idea you're passionate about, and you write an article or make a video. You include links in it, put visuals in there, and then share it.

A caveat: sharing original content is not a guarantee of success. You need to have good connections and groups that will find your content relevant and compelling. If you end up getting no comments, no likes, or no shares, you've failed. Your content didn't move anyone. It didn't engage anyone, so it didn't advance any relationship building, which is what social selling rests on.

When you make original content, you need to get comments, likes, and shares—not just views—because that means that your content actually made someone do something. Someone was inspired to say, "I disagree. These are the reasons why,", or "I agree passionately because of this and this".

That's the idea of a blog. Position yourself as a thought leader, push boundaries, challenge people, let people know what you think in a business context, and engage with their reactions—positive or negative.

It's reactions that elicit engagement and social activity. That's what you want to happen with any content marketing you do.

LinkedIn has two forms of a blog: long-form articles and short-form posts. LinkedIn used to prioritise long-form articles, but now they promote and generate views for the short form post.

Long forms are 500 to 1,000 words and can be edited down to also create a short form post of 250 words with a link back to the long form. You can also use the short form to promote outside blogs on, say, your website or a media publication.

Short posts can also be a rant or observation about a piece of curated content you're sharing or about a photo, event photo, or infographic. Short posts like this will likely get great traction, which is what you want!

You'll find a whole chapter dedicated to posting videos on LinkedIn. Very briefly, I want to mention videos here to say that they are now also key to success on LinkedIn. To truly socially sell people want to know who you are, what you want out of life, what your views are, and your mannerisms. Your personality comes across and your personal brand is communicated so effectively through videos, more than any other context and medium, which is why they are so effective and LinkedIn is pushing so hard for them. P eople buy people, and there is no better way of communicating your personal brand than video.

6: Strategically time your content sharing

The final way of content marketing is using a time-based platform like Hootsuite or Buffer to strategically time when your content will hit particular groups of people. LinkedIn has peaks and troughs in terms of when people actually view content. Normally the times' people most often use LinkedIn is in the morning on the way to work, at lunchtime, and on their way home. On top of that, people are in different time zones.

For example, I'm in Sydney now. The timezone here is different to New Zealand, which is two hours ahead and different to Singapore, where I live, which is three hours behind. When I employ this strategic timing strategy, using my Hootsuite or Buffer, I am launching my content with the aim of hitting people in these various locations at different times.

Let me add that for this strategy any type of content applies. That could be curated content, it could be photographs, it could be infographics, it could be reported, it could be blogs. It could be anything at all. The point with this strategy is that I have to think about how a user base in a particular country is accessing that content and what the benefit is to actually doing so.

I have to make that content realistic and valuable to that particular person, whether they are an entrepreneur, CEO, CMO, executive, manager, or employee, in a particular country, at a particular time. Using Buffer or Hootsuite's time-delay option is great, but you have to be thoughtful about the particular content you are releasing as well.

No matter the content marketing strategy you use, or what combo you use, they all rest on the same principle: content is at the heart of social selling. The content you and others like, share, post, create, and comment on is what allows engagement to happen. It allows you and so many others to get social with one another.

The content you choose to focus on, whether that be in terms of creating it yourself or posting it, liking it, or commenting on it—is the springboard off of which others will engage with you and vice versa. This is how relationships are built and how your social selling gets put into motion.

Because not all content is equal—some more engaging and some less—you need to take this into account when you post content. In the next chapter, I'll share the secret sauce in terms of determining when to post hard-sell type content and when to post soft-sell and no-sell content too. It all matters in keeping your social-selling mechanism running well.

Chapter 9
The Golden Ratio: 4-1-1

In the previous chapter, we talked about how your use of the content is critical in enticing engagement, relationships, and social selling. In this chapter, we're going to extend that discussion about content marketing because it's just that important. To (perhaps) state the obvious—not all content is equal in terms of being interesting to other people.

For example, if you decide to create your own content and all that content is about what an expert you are and how awesome your company is, then you can expect people are going to get bored of it pretty quickly.

It's like you are meeting someone and you two are trying to start a conversation, and all you offer is talk about your accomplishments—the other person will get bored pretty fast, even if what you are saying is true. It works the same on LinkedIn.

To make sure you stay interesting and relevant in your approach to content on LinkedIn, here's the golden ratio for social sharing.

It called the 4–1–1 social sharing strategy. What it means is that for every six pieces of content you share via social media:

- 4 pieces of content should be interesting and relevant to your audience (with *no* kind of mention of you or your company at all)
- 1 piece should be your own content that's a soft sell. You don't mention your company, but you discuss an area of your expertise and give your audience helpful info, and they can connect the dots back to you and your company.
- 1 piece is sales-related content for your product or service, e.g., a coupon, press release, limited-time offer, etc. This is your hard sell.

I'll give you a quick example to show you what I mean. For Black Marketing, we would post:

- 4 pieces of content on, say, (1) innovation in Hong Kong, (2) work-life balance, (3) off-the-beaten-track restaurant gems in Shanghai that are perfect for business lunches, and (4) advice from five people on how they stay focused and productive when working from home
- 1 piece about content marketing (which we specialise in)
- 1 piece about Black Marketing and what we do

When you do the 4–1–1, the one in six times you do offer a hard-sell post, your audience is more likely to see it. Otherwise, if you are very frequently doing hard-sell posts, your audience will unfollow you or hide your feed, and you won't know it.

So, do not just post about your company all the time. It's boring. Post about other relevant, interesting, and related issues, people, ideas, etc., to create buzz. Whether it is for your individual LinkedIn profile page or your company's, follow this 4–1–1 social sharing strategy to make sure you stay interesting to your audience.

Humdrum to Wow!

Often when HR takes over a company's LinkedIn—because they don't know about marketing; it's not what they do—they end up only posting job notices. Over and over again. But most viewers won't be interested. They want to know the strategy and ethos of a company, not a job position it has open in a branch that's nowhere near where they live.

For instance, let's take Marriott's LinkedIn. Rather than talking about their hotel, they've done a series of posts and shares about productivity. In this way, they are saying something about their brand but also offering engaging info to their audience, getting a conversation going.

If Marriott wrote about, say, a marketing assistant position available in Tampa, then their audience everywhere else in the world wouldn't care. But, if they post about work-life balance, then everyone is interested and can get engaged. This is what you want to do too: present your brand in a business context and get people to share and be engaged with what you write.

The Intersection of Business and Personal

I've been following the CNN anchor for Hong Kong Kristie Lu Stout on LinkedIn for a while, and her posts teach us a lot about content marketing. Sometimes she posts serious stuff, for instance, "Beyond Plastic," which got 64 likes, and a post about Guatemala that got 39 likes.

Interestingly, when Kristie posts personal but business-relevant stuff—her number of likes greatly increases. She wrote about Anthony Bourdain and then about Kate Spade and got 500 likes. Her most popular post is about a great weekend she spent in Hong Kong.

People are interested in what she thinks from a business perspective, and they're even more interested in her personal business perspective. They are interested in her and her personal branding, and want to engage with her—and the same applies to you.

The takeaway: don't only offer content related to your company. Follow the 4–1–1.

People Follow You, Not Your Company

In my *Personal Branding Mastery for Entrepreneurs* book I talk about how you market your brand through you. That's especially true when it comes to content. You can post all the content you like on your company page, and no one will care. Why?

Because people don't follow companies; they follow people.

When you post the content on your page or share the content from your company page on your page, then suddenly you will see massive engagement. People care and will comment, like, and share.

The amount of people that we see who complain that no one follows or shares content from their company page is astounding. Our response: we point out that they themselves and none of their C-suite are actually sharing content or even liking content or commenting on content from their company page, so how can they expect their company employees to?

So what do you do?

Lead by example and post on your page, and you will get more engagement than that of any post on your company page.

LinkedIn is not a company marketing plan. It's a personal branding marketing platform. You market your company through you.

To put it in perspective the LinkedIn company page on LinkedIn, where there are 600 million professionals all presumably who like the LinkedIn brand, only has 4 million followers. That's less than 1% of people on their own platform that bother to follow the actual brand itself on the same platform.

Jeff Weiner, CEO of LinkedIn has 9 million followers, more than twice as many as the company that made him famous.

Google only has 8 million and is the top page followed on LinkedIn. Compare this to one of the top influencers on LinkedIn: Richard Branson. He has 16 million followers. Richard Branson (= person) has twice as many followers as Google (=company).

Apple and Amazon, the top two most valuable companies in the world, only have 5 million followers each. Facebook only 3 million. Even Microsoft, which owns LinkedIn, only has 6 million followers. Compare the number of followers of these major companies to the number one influencer on LinkedIn: Bill Gates. He has 18 million followers.

People follow people.

People follow people's content.

More than an Upgrade

Here's a final example that shows the awesome power of offering interesting content that isn't hard- or soft-selling your business. The back story: I was at the Ritz-Carlton in Hong Kong, but my room wasn't yet ready. I contacted management and let them know that I had intended to use it as a space for meetings, so I needed a temporary meeting space. At no additional charge, they offered me one of their boardrooms—not just for a few hours or even a day, but for the whole week!

At the end of that first day, I did a short post on my LinkedIn about customer service and customer experience, both of which the Ritz-Carlton is big on. I also included of photo of myself in a Back in Black AC/DC t-shirt, sitting on the boardroom table and looking very happy.

A day later, my post had 54,000 views (I'd expected, maybe 1,000). Ricco De Blank, the CEO of Ritz-Carlton, read my post and requested a meeting with me.

The result: Ricco became a Black Marketing client and the Ritz-Carlton became one as well. My post wasn't even a hard sell, it didn't mention my company or what we did once. It wasn't any kind of sell at all, but it created so much engagement and conversation that it set the social selling machine in motion. Let's remember this for our future posts!

The next chapter continues this foray into the content side of social selling in a discussion of videos. In particular, you posting original videos on your LinkedIn to engage people with your personal brand.

Chapter 10
Video: Critical to Social Selling

As I've shared in the previous two chapters, at the heart of social selling you'll find content.

First, you offer compelling, relevant content, some from others on LinkedIn, some from outside sources, and some that you originate. From there, others become engaged with you and you build relationships, which can lead to sales and recommendations for sales.

As I'll explain in more detail in the next chapter (about the 1–9–90), it is essential that you create and offer original content. When the content comes from you, you make yourself more than a follower or sharer—you make yourself a thought leader. A decision-maker. You increase your credibility.

Video's Supremacy

In terms of creating your own content, the most effective at increasing your social selling is videos. When you make videos, you not only share relevant advice and information, but you also share yourself—your personality, expertise, authenticity, and style.

Building relationships is an essential element in social selling, so the more others can engage with you as a whole person, the more social selling happens. Much more so than your original blogs, photographs, or infographics, a video is the medium that most fully portrays you as an authentic, complete, and professional person.

Video is key in terms of getting across your personality across, your personal branding, your energy, and your ideas. A video is fabulous in terms of allowing you to offer simple ideas about different things, whether it's interesting takes from a conference, you interviewing fascinating people, or you offering helpful advice.

For example, I recently made a short video celebrating my ten years on LinkedIn. I offered ten tips for those ten years. I posted the video on a Sunday, and it got around 20,000 views. So many people commented, "That's fantastic! Amazing!"

Something to note about my example: I strategically timed its release—a Sunday—because I learnt that many people, like entrepreneurs, use LinkedIn on Saturdays and Sundays. Multinationals don't work weekends or public holidays so take advantage of this by getting greater cut-through and posting at times when others are not.

Quick review: when you post great content and you're strategic about when you time its release, you get more engagement.

LinkedIn's Latest Obsession

Currently, LinkedIn is obsessed with encouraging its users to post videos. It's a new feature that LinkedIn recently put in place, so it makes sense they're so gung-ho about it. LinkedIn offers users the option to upload videos that are, at most, ten minutes long. It has a cap at ten minutes and won't allow you to post a video that is beyond the 9:59-minute mark.

From my experience, I recommend videos in the two- to four-minute range. Additionally, you can input keywords and subtitles. In this way, your videos allow you to actually sell, sell, sell your personality and your authentic brand as you give away genuinely helpful and interesting tips.

Videos don't need to be Hollywood productions either. In fact, LinkedIn users like authentic, rough-and-ready videos. So use your mobile and shoot it free-flow, just getting across some simple facts and thoughts, and you'll be amazed how well your audience loves it and loves your authenticity.

Spontaneous, fallible, enthusiastic, and respectful of viewers' time are all key as is the fact that you should look as if you are enjoying yourself! Talk with passion about your business, what you do or with other people about their business, and their passion.

Then share and tag relevant people that you think would be interested. When you tag someone, they get a notification about you mentioning them and they look at your video/post and hopefully share, like, and comment, thus getting your content into their feed with their followers and hopefully—beyond.

YouTube vs. LinkedIn—And the Winner Is . . .

When I do my masterclasses, I video them and post them on my YouTube channel. Then I share those links on LinkedIn. Normally these videos are two to five minutes each. I've got a series of them on LinkedIn and a series on YouTube.

However, I want to point out that YouTube and LinkedIn are not equal in terms of social selling. I don't find YouTube nearly as helpful as LinkedIn because YouTube (or Vimeo) doesn't offer select data on who's viewing my videos and profile.

LinkedIn allows you data that you can look at and parse to learn a lot about your audience. On LinkedIn, you can tell who viewed your profile as a result of watching your video; who liked, commented, and shared as a result of seeing your video; who liked the video itself; and who commented on the video itself.

Being able to determine more about individual audience members is necessary if you want to start engaging with them individually and then build relationships with each person. Remember, social selling is social. It's all about social engagement. When you make and post a video, ultimately you want it to lead to sales—and for that to happen, you have to engage with viewers. LinkedIn's unique data offerings allow you to do that!

The next chapter continues our study of content marketing in its look at the 1—9—90, which, as you'll soon see, is all about positioning yourself as a thought leader. If you are posting videos of yourself, as I've recommended in this chapter that you do, then you're already making yourself into a thought leader, which is essential for increasing the reach of your social selling.

Chapter 11

1-9-90: Engage, Don't Just Watch

Join the 1%. Be an influencer. Shine as the expert you are. Show yourself as a leader. That's essential to your social selling success. And it's what this chapter is all about. Let's look at what I'm talking about.

The 1–9–90

Through a lot of stats and research, experts found that of all the participants on social media, only 1% create and lead. It's that 1% who are writing blogs, doing videos, and posting original and curated content.

The next important finding: only 9% of participants then share, like, and comment on content. We need these essential people for our content to go viral.

The final finding: a whopping 90% of participants do nothing. They do absolutely nothing. They only view—they view, they view, they view.

This is the 1–9–90:

1% are the leaders; 9% the active responders; and 90% the silent viewers. I'm going to show you how to leverage this finding to optimise your social selling.

To achieve optimal social selling, you must leverage the 1–9–90 on your LinkedIn. What does this mean? It means that you become the 1% and post original content on LinkedIn. From there, 9% of folks viewing will engage with your content, so you must be ready to interact with them.

And you can expect 90% of people to silently view your content and not actively respond—but they still matter. They matter a lot. They are viewing and getting influenced both by the original content you post and by your level of engagement with the 9%.

The 1

Most importantly, you need to be leading and influencing by joining that 1% and posting original content. By joining this 1%, you move from follower to leader. You're actually dictating what's being said, what's being read, and what's being engaged with. You're provoking people, putting stuff out there, which, in effect, shows off you and your personal brand.

Your original content serves as a kind of marketing of yourself and your business; you are soft selling yourself through it even when you don't mention yourself or your company. You will have a greater share of voice, which leads to more sales when you make the effort to create original content and put yourself in the 1%. Unsurprisingly, the better your quality of content, the more beneficial it will be to you and your bottom line.

The 9

You need the 9%, who are your key followers. So it's crucial to engage with your followers. That's why I like, share, and thank every single person who comments on any of my original content, whether it be videos, long posts, shorts posts, curated content. Anything. Also, I interact with anyone who tags me.

I thank them for tagging me, I share, like, and answer their questions because I know to optimise my social selling, I must always be engaging, engaging, engaging. Engaging equates to building relationships, which, along with content, lies at the foundation of social selling.

The 90

Engaging with that 9% is key to your success. Because you don't know the 90% who are anonymously viewing, you can't directly engage with them. Leveraging the 1–9–90 is all about using the 1% by becoming a part of the 1% and leading.

Then you need the 9% to help you engage the 90%. If you don't have the 9%, you can't engage the 90% because that 90% is viewing and noting all the engagement between you and the 9%, i.e., the active responders.

So social media, whether it's LinkedIn, YouTube, Facebook, Instagram, or WeChat, is all about the 1% engaging with the 9% to disseminate information to the 90%. In doing so, we in the 1% get our social selling machine churning to compel, entice, inspire, and vouch for our credibility, influence, expertise, and leadership, for the 99% (9% + 90%) who are engaging with or silently viewing what we have to offer.

Leverage this 1–9–90 to increase your reach and grow your business. It's what social selling is all about!

In the next chapter we'll explore the role of influence on social selling, so you can see that when you join the 1% and create original content, it will position you as an influencer to your audience.

Chapter 12

Influence and Social Selling: Here's the Deal

Are influences good or bad for social selling? From all you've learned so far, you should already know the answer: influence is key for social selling, particularly in the B2B space. Influence in the B2B space is paramount.

Whether it's a Richard Branson, Arne Sorenson, Candice Galek, or Ricco De Blank—there are lots of influencers on LinkedIn. They're influencing people through their authentic stories of leadership and employer branding. You can judge them in terms of their content, connections, followers, reputation, and what they've done.

A Potent Example of Far-Reaching B2B Influence

Let's take a look at the impressive influence of Ricco De Blank, the CEO of a massive hotel chain in Asia, who owns businesses like the Ritz-Carlton in Shanghai and Hong Kong. On his LinkedIn, Ricco talks about how his ten years working directly for the Ritz-Carlton helped him to gain critical insights into exemplary customer experience and customer service.

That's the ultimate in social selling because when he's passing on information about amazing customer service that's he's garnered from his work at the Ritz-Carlton, including the levels they expect from both employers, employees, and their leaders, all of this interests his followers—all of whom are potential B2B and B2C clients.

Not only are Ricco De Blank's followers learning from him about how to improve their own customer service, at the same time he is influencing them to expect this top-notch customer experience and service at his hotels, like the Ritz-Carlton.

As they view his videos and read his blog posts, his followers are thinking, "Wow, this is amazing. This is Ricco De Blank talking about how phenomenal customer experience and service happens as he's learned it at the Ritz-Carlton. Not only can I implement his advice at my business, but something else: I know I'm going to get phenomenal service at the Ritz-Carlton. I want to bring a client there, or a date there, because I know they're going to be impressed. Hey, I might have a conference at the Ritz-Carlton because I know that it's going to be stunning, complete with a stunning backdrop and stunning customer service. And I know that the Ritz-Carlton will do absolutely everything I need. I love that".

In this way, Ricco De Blank is offering authentic observations and advice that will help other business leaders grow their businesses. At the same time he's social selling his own businesses. He's putting it out there in terms of what the Ritz-Carlton believes, its ethos.

It's known too that Apple has taken a ton of Ricco De Blank's recommendations and put them into practice in their customer experience and service. Talk about increasing his credibility by having Apple take his advice and join his following. That's some serious influence!

Branson's Influence on Black Marketing

I've seen Richard Branson do the same kind of effective influencing as well. For example, Richard Branson talks about how a key to his businesses' success depends on retaining talented employees because talented employees are key to retaining customers. In places like Singapore and Hong Kong where there is a shortage of talent, this is especially true.

The following is an attitude and practice Richard Branson recommends repeatedly in his videos and blogs: "When you are a happy employee, you will make our clients happy. If you're a miserable employee, then you are not going to make our clients happy. Therefore, you need to be happy first. I need you to be happy with the work conditions."

Richard Branson has influenced me about the running of my business, Black Marketing. He's helped me to realize that you can't get a writer to write when they don't feel like writing; you can't get a musician to make music when they don't feel like it. And that's often not at Monday at 9 o'clock in the morning.

This is how Richard Branson's influence in this area has permeated how I run Black Marketing. At Black Marketing, to help employees be happy, we offer flexible working hours and locations. My employees can work from home, at Starbucks, in co-working spaces, or at the office.

They can come in when they want and leave when they want. They can take Fridays off and work Saturdays; they can work the weekend and not work the week. As long as they deliver the key performance indicators (KPIs) to our clients, I don't care when or where they do their work.

For them to deliver KPIs, they must be happy. Deciding their own schedules and places for doing work means they'll be most creative and happy when they are working, which is essential for them to do amazing work.

Influence is key to social selling because I've gotten a very positive impression of Richard Branson's businesses based on the advice he gives on his blogs and videos on LinkedIn. In turn, I am recommending him and his businesses to my colleagues, LinkedIn connections, and everyone reading this book, and I'm engaging with his businesses as well. This is classic social selling, both B2B, and B2C, happening due to influence.

Similarly, I get an impression of the Ritz-Carlton and how Ricco runs his hotels through his blogging and his ethos, and I can relate it back to what I see every single time I actually experience the Ritz-Carlton. Again, this is influence leading to successful social selling.

Arne Soreson's Influence on Hospitality Social Selling

Arene Sorenson is an inspirational LinkedIn leader, who leads by example. He blogs about things that matter to him and that he is passionate about. His passion for his employees and his business really shines through in his content. He blogs about being a leader, and about

Bill Marriott, the founder of the hotel chain that he now is CEO for, the largest in the world.

Arne talks about customer service, immigration, hot topics that he knows his stakeholders will rise to and respect on LinkedIn. All his stakeholders are on LinkedIn, from his employees to his shareholders, his clients for MICE, his clients for rooms, his clients for B2B and B2C, and his clients for all food and beverage, from corporate dining to casual drinks with partners, colleagues, peers, and clients.

By writing so prolifically and passionately on LinkedIn Arne is communicating both his brand values and those of his company to all of these stakeholders. My view of Marriott certainly has changed as a result of reading his blogs. This is classic content marketing: simple, compelling, free, and all the while effectively socially selling Arne's business, the Marriott.

Influence in the B2C Space

From my explanation and examples, it's apparent that influence in B2B, particularly on LinkedIn, is absolutely crucial. What about influence in the B2C space—is it as powerful?

For influence to work in the B2C space, the influencer has to be very genuine, or it just won't work. To narrow down what I mean, for example, a person can't be selling or promoting one product one minute and then another product the next minute, and expect their influence to work on both (or all) products.

It won't work. It'll come off as disingenuous. They'll come off as a sellout, pushing products just because they get paid to, which means people won't believe them.

People often forget that B2B buyers are also B2C buyers, and you know that they are white-collar and affluent because they are on LinkedIn and you can see where they work and who they are. If someone stays at a hotel for business, it's also an opportunity to sell them a consumer product for that birthday or anniversary or gift for themselves or someone else. LinkedIn works the same way.

The Makings of an Influencer

Every single leader out there is an influencer. Why? Because leaders are the people stepping up and putting themselves out there when they offer original content in videos, blogs, short posts, and infographics. As I've been saying repeatedly in this book, when you join that 1% that actually offers original content on social media, you put yourself in a leadership position.

You are voicing to the 99% following you (remember, 1–9–90?)— 9% of whom will engage with you and 90% of whom will just quietly view—what you actually believe in. Your voice, ideas, and personality, thus, pervade through to your followers' organizations. In this way, you are influencing them and their organizations.

These people are leading their organizations, so they're deciding, based on your influence, what their organizations should and should not buy.

When I talk about the Ritz-Carlton, I'm an influencer for the Ritz-Carlton. I'm helping to promote them by discussing my great experiences I've had with them. If I've had a bad experience somewhere, I might write a bad review for the place on TripAdvisor. In this way, I'm an influencer as well.

The point: when we take the time to voice ourselves and post original content, we become influencers. We can all become influencers, and we all should as it will help us tremendously with social selling, especially when we use our influence over LinkedIn.

In the next chapter, we'll explore Sales Navigator, LinkedIn's premium search engine. You'll learn how to target the most promising potential leads to spread your influence to them in a carefully-crafted way.

Chapter 13

Sales Navigator: Your Social Selling Optimiser

At the end of the day, LinkedIn is a social media platform. It's how you leverage the platform that will make the difference in achieving your social selling goals. LinkedIn actually offers some special software, Sales Navigator, specifically developed to enhance users' abilities to socially sell on LinkedIn—and I can't urge you enough to take advantage of all that Sales Navigator has to offer.

What It Is

LinkedIn's Sales Navigator is an advanced sales tool that helps you build and nurture relationships on LinkedIn. As you know, social selling stems from personal relationships, so from the particular people and businesses Sales Navigator helps you locate and the relationships you build with them, the more sales will result.

With the highly refined searches Sales Navigator allows you to perform, you can locate the kind of people who would most likely be interested in you and your service or product. Sales Navigator allows you special access to information and insights about these leads, so you can understand them better and use that to shape your engagement with them, making it more personal and relevant.

As Diana Kucer, LinkedIn's director of global product marketing, explained, "Sales Navigator allows sales professionals to tap into the power of LinkedIn efficiently. It improves social selling in support of powerful daily habits".

Prized Insights and Info

The data that Sales Navigator allows you to access is fantastic. It tells you who's active on LinkedIn (as opposed to people who appear on LinkedIn but their accounts are dormant) because you only want to spend time targeting people who are active on LinkedIn.

It also tells who is a premium member, who is open profile, and how many shared connections you both have in common, all essential data that tells you that the person will at least see a message you send them. From there, it's down to you to make a compelling case for them to answer it.

Sales Navigator allows you to do highly narrow searches, with particular filters for "people" and "company" searches. "People" search filters include industry, company size, role in a company, interests, postal code, seniority level, school, and more. "Company" search filters include company headcount, revenue, size, industry, and relationship (companies where your connections work), and more.

You can also do keyword searches and language searches amongst other things, like groups and how long someone has been at their current role. All the data is available.

Sales Navigator is the trump card over any other social media platform like Twitter, Facebook, WeChat, Instagram, etc., in that they do not offer you access to this data. None of it.

The great thing about building target lists on LinkedIn is that are saved (and you can do fifteen of these), and once you have built them they will start generating daily leads for you. How does this work? For example, I could make target list with the following parameters: second connections who are founders of mid-sized companies (companies with 11 to 50 employees), in Singapore, in the marketing industry, with 10-plus years of experience, more than three years at that company, and who are active on LinkedIn. Next, LinkedIn will give me an initial list.

Once that list is saved, then LinkedIn will give me new leads based on this criteria. This works by LinkedIn finding people daily who have just joined LinkedIn or just moved to Singapore or just become active. It also works when you connect with someone. Once you are connected, you get access to that person's first connections, and if any fulfill this criteria, then LinkedIn informs me. That's why you need to have lots of connections in the community that you wish to target to get leads (we cover this in detail in chapter 15).

Entrepreneurs know other entrepreneurs. When you connect with someone that has 5,000 connections in Hong Kong or Sydney, then suddenly you have hundreds of potential new leads of second connections (i.e., the first connections of the person you connect with become your second connections) who are entrepreneurs in those cities. It all happens through that one connect. LinkedIn gives you regular reports about these people if you have saved the right list to capture them.

Sales Navigator will also use all it knows about you and your activity on LinkedIn to recommend people to you that it thinks you could build a profitable relationship with—and these recommendations are surprisingly good!

LinkedIn will also tell you over Sales Navigator who has been in the news. It'll let you know who has changed jobs. This is information that you could use to message those people and congratulate them about. It even helps you figure out if any of your connections' connections fit the criteria to be great clients for you.

Sales Navigator also tells you who is sharing the same passion as you by sharing the same group. They you can message someone saying just that, that you share the same group and it makes sense to explore the possibility of working together.

If you opt for the premium level of Sales Navigator, it will actually show you the people and companies who have visited your profile. Then you can use the InMail, open profile, or first degree feature to begin engaging with them.

Open profiles are the secret sauce of LinkedIn. Only on Sales Navigator can you tell who is open profile. Then you can send them a free—yes free—LinkedIn message on Sales Navigator. If you combine the knowledge through the data that you have about these people, then you can have a great success rate of people actually seeing your message and responding. And you should already know why this is crucial—it's the backbone of social selling. Back-and-forth engagement and relationship building make the social selling wheels turn.

Scripts

It's all very well having a great list, but data is useless if you have an incomplete LinkedIn profile, such as no photo or no summary or no company description or no content marketing. Make sure all of this is in order before you send a message to a potential client.

Once all that is in order, then it's time to craft your script. When I say "script", I'm referring to the initial message you send to a prospect to get a relationship started with them. A great list of ideal prospects is useless if your script is terrible or too long—or too long and terrible! LinkedIn advises the shorter the better. You need a good headline. You need to personalise the headline and the main message, and include a compelling call to action that is simple to understand.

"Visiting Hong Kong" is one of my most effective headlines. Next I make the body of my message about how I would love to help the person with their personal branding, LinkedIn ,and marketing, and would love to meet them during a limited period only. Simple, short, and to the point, respecting someone's time.

A script like this is effective because it creates a short window of opportunity to meet, gives a reason, and communicates the point simply and briefly. I then put my credentials at the bottom, not in the main body of the message. Remember, this message is about them, the person you are writing to.

Another great thing to do is point out how you can help them. Personalise it.

Also mention people that you both know, which could be peers, clients, or alumni from business school. Any form of personlisation is effective in social selling success.

Personalise, personalise, personalise. Social selling is just that social, so make it personal.

Saving Leads

Sales Navigator also allows you to save leads. Once they are saved you can track all their activity, this includes:

- their shared content, which you can like, share, and comment, and they will get a notification saying that this has happened
- when they appear in the news
- when they change jobs
- when they view your profile
- when their company is in the news
- what their company is sharing

These people do not know that you have saved them as a lead. They just know that you're being very attentive to them. Because they see that they are on your radar, you then get on their radar, which makes them more open to taking the time to read a message from you, respond to that message, and then build a relationship and potentially a partnership. This is social selling.

LinkedIn will also suggest leads for you based on the leads that you share, and you can start following them, saving them, and engaging with them.

Notifications

In my first book, *LinkedIn Mastery for Entrepreneurs*, I talk about how you need to maximise your headline to make it work for you. It works by letting the receiver immediately know what you do. It works by allowing you to be found through a keyword search, and it works by appearing everywhere that you do, from searches to other people's profiles and all your content.

If your headline is well crafted and communicates what you do effectively and succinctly, then every notification that you send is socially selling you.

More on Scripts

LinkedIn gives you all the data of when people are doing things from when they start a new job to their work anniversary, from when they view your profile to when they comment/share/like your content. You must be ready when this happens.

Prepare scripts which you can adapt and personalise to each occasion that both engage the receiver and sell you at the same time.

For example, on your "congratulations script", say congratulations to them about their new role or their anniversary, and then point out that if they would like to talk about their personal branding or LinkedIn marketing, that now would be a great time to do so. In this way, you're selling by complimenting, then selling. Again, this is social selling.

In summary: Sales Navigator offers you a way to get ahead in terms of lead generation, personal branding, connecting, and targeting the right kind of people. Use Sales Navigator to optimise your ability to socially sell over LinkedIn. I can't recommend it enough.

While you might think that your high quality work speaks for itself, for social selling to happen you actually need other people—lots of other people—to be talking about you and your high quality work. As we'll cover in the next chapter, it's not what you know but *who* you know that allows your social selling to get going and stay going.

Chapter 14

It's Not What You Know.
It's Who You Know.

Seeing as social selling is social, resting on engaging with others and building relationships, the topic of this chapter should make sense to you: it's not what you know but *who* you know that determines your success in social selling on LinkedIn.

If you are an expert in your field who offers phenomenal services or sells a premium product, but you only have five connections on LinkedIn, then LinkedIn won't work for you. You must make connections. It's all about connections: first, second, third, and group connections.

Growing Your Reach

I run into people frequently who are not interested in making connections on LinkedIn. The fact is, not making connections with people means missing the whole point of LinkedIn. When you connect to someone who has 30,000 connections, you gain access to their 30,000 connections and all their first and second connections, so you're gaining millions of new people in your network—what a treasure trove!

When you connect to others on LinkedIn, they become your first connections, their first connections become your second connections, and their second connections become your third connections. So, just by connecting with one other person, who has, say, 30,000 connections, you suddenly have 30,001 second connections who can lead you to millions more third connections. That's a ton of people to have the opportunity to start engaging with and social selling to.

For example, in Singapore, I have 10,500 first connections. This, in turn, leads me to have half a million second connections, and 1.5 million third connections. That means I can target two million connections in Singapore, out of the 2.3 million people in Singapore on LinkedIn. Imagine my reach when I repeat that in Sydney, Hong Kong, London, Zurich, Shanghai, Melbourne, and basically all the cities where Black Marketing has clients and I am targeting people . . .

Growing your number of connections, whether it be first, second, or third connections, is critical to social selling. If you want to influence people and reach out to people socially, you need your first connections to share you and your content with their first connections, which makes their first connections your second connections.

You need their second connections sharing you and your content, which could transform them into your first connections. In this way, your influence grows exponentially, which should result in a noticeable increase in your social selling. It's all about three degrees of separation. It's all about connections, connections, connections—who you know, not what you know.

Social Selling Reassurance

I'm in the entrepreneurial community and the marketing community. When I connect with CEOs, influencers, and entrepreneurs, I know that they can connect me to others in their communities. I have to make sure to broaden my base of connections to leverage this power of people connecting people. It's not so they can recommend me, not really. It's about how somebody who's my second or third connection can see that we have many mutual connections.

When they see this, they're much more likely to respond to a message from me on LinkedIn or engage with me on LinkedIn. When I reach out and go, "I'd love to meet you. We both have 1,000 connections in common in the entrepreneurial marketing space," then they are more likely to be open to me.

The more shared connections you have with someone else, the more open they will be to building a relationship with you, which could lead to you making sales. That is social selling reassurance. We both know hundreds of the same people; therefore, we're in the same space; therefore, it's justification to at least engage, read a message.

Additionally, when you do engage a second or third connection, in addition to drawing their attention to the many mutual connections you share, be sure that your message is personal to them. Use Sales Navigator to learn about them and their business, and when you engage with them, show your genuine interest and concern in them. We covered this several times already in the book and there's still a chapter coming up, chapter 18, devoted to personalisation because it's just that important and effective.

Making connections on LinkedIn is crucial to making use of the platform. The more people you know, the more potential relationships you can build, thus the more social selling you can accomplish.

Because the topic of connections is so critical to your social selling success, we're going to continue the discussion in the next chapter where we'll focus on growing your number of first connections.

Chapter 15
An Abundance of First Connections

An intrinsic element to social selling on LinkedIn is having many, many first connections. Numerous first connections allow you more opportunities to socially sell. If you don't have lots of first connections, it doesn't work. To explain, let me give you an example.

A business came to Black Marketing and told us their problem: "We've got a whole team using Sales Navigator just like we've seen you recommend in your videos, but it doesn't seem to be working. Our social selling hasn't taken off. What do you think is the problem?"

In response, we checked out their LinkedIn profiles. What we found was that each member of their team had less than one hundred connections. Once we saw this, we immediately knew this was the problem. If you have one hundred or less first connections, that's too few for social selling to take off. Why?

For social selling to work, you depend on your first connections' first connections (your second connections) and your first connections' first connections' first connections (your third connections). The more connections your first connections have, then the more leads you have to influence and potentially connect with. The same goes for third connections.

So, if you only have one hundred first connections, then it is most likely you'll only have 1,000 second connections and, maybe, 10,000 third connections. Frankly, that's just not enough for Sales Navigator to draw from to allow you optimal results.

Sales Navigator needs a very large pool to draw from for your social selling to take off. You need (1) many, many first connections, and (2) those first connections should be of high quality (meaning, they should be well connected themselves, thus offering you a massive pool of second and third connections).

The Key: The Second

Second connections are key to successful social selling and optimising what Sales Navigator can offer you. Here's why: in general in life, we are more open to new people when they offer us someone that we both have in common. People are more open to us when we introduce ourselves and let them know from the start someone or some people that we both have in common.

The same is true with social selling on LinkedIn. You need lots of second connections because those are the folks you'll look to engage with, and you'll have a better chance of that engagement happening if you're connected to the same people. And, obviously, those second connections can lead you to third connections when it comes to influence.

Big Influence

The way you get something to go viral on LinkedIn (which makes you, your brand, and your service or product known) is to actually entice your first connections with impressive content that they'll share with their first connections who will then share it with their first connections, etc. That way you're hitting first, second, and third connections.

Therefore, your content is being influential, it's being shared by people on LinkedIn who basically are in your same area of business. In Black Marketing's case, this means CEOs, entrepreneurs, and marketers. You have to have many, many, many first connections (and high-quality ones, at that) for this to happen.

High Quantity and Quality

The most first connections LinkedIn allows any one profile to have is 30,000. I hit that limit four years ago. Basically, once you hit that limit you have to delete and add, delete and add, delete and add. Once you hit that limit, your strategy becomes acquiring the highest quality first connections possible.

I don't want 30,000 first connections that have only one or two connections to offer me. I'm looking for 30,000 first connections who ultimately have reached the 30,000 limit themselves. They are the ones who have the most to offer me, and I to them.

I'll give you a great example. Say, I target a city where Black Marketing doesn't yet have a lot of clients. Let's say, Brisbane. If I want to set up a lot of meetings there, I need to quickly build up my number of entrepreneur first connections there.

To do this I will reach out to some entrepreneurs there, sending them personalised messages, citing particular first connections we have in common in Sydney or Melbourne, cities where I do have lots of first connections. I might write, "You know this particular person in Sydney. She's the first connection of yours, you're my second connection now. Let's meet".

In this way, my first connections supply me with second connections, thus giving me automatic credibility and an opening to the second connections. Ultimately I can meet up with those second connections and either do business with them, or they can introduce me to other relevant connections whom I might do business with.

Using this method, very quickly I could have 1,000 connections (who had been second connections but whom I converted to first) in Brisbane. Next, through these new first connections, I could reach tens of thousands of entrepreneurs in Brisbane, the Gold Coast, and the Sunshine Coast.

Even though I started with zero leads in Brisbane, after using Sales Navigator's refined search options and the second connections' first connections that we have in common, I could tap into a vast community of entrepreneurs in the Brisbane area of Australia and begin relationships with potential new clients.

I also don't want 30,000 connections who have thousands of connections but who don't engage on LinkedIn, don't share, or even check their feeds. High quality connections are people who both have lots of the right kind of connections and also who are active on LinkedIn. The reason it makes a difference that they are active on LinkedIn is that when you make contact with any of their connections, because they are so active, then they are well-known and appreciated by their second connections; thus, their second connection will value the fact that you both share a connection to this one person. In this way, a person with lots of connections on LinkedIn and who is active and engaging with their connections is the Holy Grail of a connection.

The objective of social selling is to meet people, talk, and see how you can do business together. When you have a reference point from a first connection, second connections are much more likely to do business with you. They will still check out your personal branding, your content marketing, your company, and socially research you.

But ultimately, if you have first connections who basically are connected to you and that particular person (the second connection), and you use the refined search features of Sales Navigator, social selling works well. The key: lots of first connections, who have lots and lots and lots of second connections, and who are active with their connections.

A great way to impress and entice second connections, or anyone that you reach out to on LinkedIn, is to send them a message through LinkedIn's PointDrive. PointDrive is the topic of the next chapter.

Chapter 16
Another Power Tool: PointDrive

Over and over again I've reiterated that social selling is social. It's about building relationships with other people and starting conversations about how your businesses could learn from one another and possibly even work together. The less generic and more personal and authentic your contact is, the more open the other person will be to starting a conversation, building a relationship, and even working together.

LinkedIn developed PointDrive to help users share information with prospective buyers in a more interesting and personal way. On top of that, PointDrive also enables the user to measure the prospect's interest in the sent information.

I'm going to explain it all in more detail, so you can see how using PointDrive in combination with Sales Navigator will allow you to target and deliver a more compelling, personal, and relevant message to the decision-makers you are seeking.

Easy, Elegant, Streamlined

LinkedIn explains PointDrive really well, so I'm going to explain it similarly. Imagine you've used Sales Navigator and it's helped you identify a company that you'd never considered before but that could very likely be in need of your product or service.

Using Sales Navigator, you find someone in that company whom you share a connection with. After following them for a time, noticing their interests and activity, sharing and commenting at times too, you make contact and begin exchanging some messages with them.

Imagine your exchange is going well. Next, imagine that person asking you for more information about your product or service. One option would be to send a message to them that contains some PDF attachments and links to videos and other pages on your website.

The problem is that a message like that can be overwhelming to receive. It's not user-friendly. Then, because that person can't unilaterally make a decision, they must forward on the email and attachments to several others—and the email gets even more cumbersome as it's passed along.

On your end, you don't know if what you've sent is even interesting to them. You also don't know who else is looking at it.

The great thing about PointDrive is it anticipates all this and addresses these issues so that both you and your prospect are happy with your package of information.

The Data Advantage

PointDrive allows you to package your various mediums of content—decks, generic and specific decks, videos, charts, graphs, photos, text, etc.—in a single, streamlined, and elegant way. When the PointDrive package is received, the viewing experience is organised and easy to manage for your prospect.

More importantly, you can track your prospect's engagement with the package you sent via PointDrive, and you can track who else in that business also engages with the package. This is important because it can help you identify who all is in the decision-making pool.

Let me give you an example. Say, I send a message out to you. I would include a deck or a video, for example, in the PointDrive package. Because Black Marketing can't use before-and-after examples (those are confidential), what I include in my deck are people and businesses that recommend Black Marketing.

I have 650 LinkedIn recommendations on my PointDrive, at the time of writing this book. I can tell every single person who's actually clicked on any particular link in that PointDrive deck. More importantly, I can tell exactly how many pages they downloaded and how many pages they viewed. If it's a video, I can see how many minutes they viewed. LinkedIn will even tell me which page numbers (if it's a document) they viewed.

LinkedIn will inform me, "Juan has looked at pages 16 to 24". Next, I'd look at pages 16 to 24 and realise, "Juan is interested in this particular aspect of my business". From here, I could approach Juan, and say, "I see you downloaded my PointDrive. I see you're particularly interested in pages 16 to 24, which address this particular product. Would you like to have a conversation about that product?"

Juan might very well respond, saying, "Absolutely fantastic. I was researching your product, and I'm very impressed by it. I like the fact that you've got recommendations for your product and service. I'd like to talk to you about how we can work together".

Remember, the important role of researching before buying? It's something we covered in chapter 2. People make buying decisions based on their social research in today's social media age. Since people's own research is so important, when you supply them a carefully crafted package about your business, product, service, etc., then you are the one in the driver's seat, dispensing the very information that they'll use in their research about you.

This is a great place to be! This is the place to be to decidedly set yourself up in their eyes as an expert, someone who is capable, responsible, and who delivers. Also, you can give out the contact information of others who recommend you. PointDrive's thorough and selective packaging puts you at a tremendous advantage.

With PointDrive you get access to data tracking their response to your information. This is data you can't get anywhere else. Even LinkedIn's SlideShare (which is very similar to PowerPoint) doesn't allow you to determine if a particular person has actually downloaded and spent time on your slideshow. YouTube is frustrating because, while it's great that I can see how many people have watched my videos, it doesn't tell me who exactly those people are and how much of the video they watched.

PointDrive, however, shows me who is viewing my video. That's absolutely key. I can tell how many minutes they viewed, and I can tell which aspects they're particularly interested in. It will even show me other people in their business who are viewing the video (and give me particular info on how these others are viewing it). With all this data, I am positioned to start a more personal, focused conversation.

I can share Point Drive on every script that I send out on LinkedIn, not just on Sales Navigator. I can use it on my congratulations scripts and use it to determine who viewed my profile scripts, InMails, open profile messages, and everything. I can share it in my content marketing strategy and track who has viewed it has a result of that. I can include it on my profile and drive traffic that way.

I can also include it off LinkedIn. I have my PointDrive link on my emails so that I can drive people from outside LinkedIn to my PointDrive and track that activity.

Social selling is all about engaging, getting social, and building relationships. LinkedIn's all about engaging, getting social, building relationships, and doing it all in a business context. LinkedIn and social selling go hand-in-hand.

With its software offerings, such as Sales Navigator and PointDrive, LinkedIn enables more personal, more focused, and more relevant engagement to happen from the start. Sales Navigator and PointDrive are power tools in that they allow social engagement to happen more efficiently, which helps everyone.

Concerning the content and messages you share with prospects using PointDrive or other mediums offered on LinkedIn, for any of it to carry interest and meaning, it must be authentic. You must be authentic. In the next chapter, we explore the significance of authenticity in social selling.

Chapter 17

Authenticity: Critical to Social Selling Success

As we've discussed, in social selling you share content, comment on content, and create and disseminate your own original content, all for the sake of having conversations with others, engaging together and building relationships, many of which will lead to discussions about working together. In order for your socialising to lead to any engagement, it has to be authentic. And in order for you to close a deal, you certainly have to be authentic too.

Authenticity, Impossible to Fake

In social selling, authenticity cannot be faked. For someone to be interested in you, your business, your original and shared content, you must be your real self. You must write, talk, and be who you are at your most comfortable and passionate for any of it to compel someone else to want to take the time to engage with you.

If you come off as faking your interest in a product or a person, trying to be funny or gregarious, or putting on a passion for a subject (that you honestly don't really understand or aren't too interested in), other people will sense it in less than a second.

Just because social selling happens over the internet doesn't mean people lose their keen ability to differentiate authenticity versus pretending. It works just the same as in real life. Only those who are genuine get anywhere.

You genuinely have to come across as you are. That's why it's worked so well for me to sport my Mohawk, ripped jeans, rock t-shirts, and so forth—because that's authentically me, I'm being myself. I'm at my most comfortable and inspired like this.

Actually, if I were wearing a pricey custom-made Italian suit with Ferragamo loafers, I imagine I'd come across unsure of myself because that's not me. I'm not comfortable in that get-up.

I am truly passionate about Black Marketing and the services we provide people. I'm passionate about all that LinkedIn offers to grow our businesses, our brands, our connections, and our sales. And because this is true and real for me, when I communicate it to others, they don't question my authenticity.

In fact, my authenticity is so great that it adds to my brand and my ability to socially sell. That's what I want for you too.

Let me tell you more about how authenticity-in-action has played out in my life and business: I test everything about LinkedIn and social selling on my profile first. If it works there, then the team learns it and brings it to our clients. Nothing goes out without being tested on my profile first. That's a first-rate example of authenticity.

The reason I started a LinkedIn marketing agency to in the first place was because I didn't know anyone in Asia. When I first came to Singapore I knew no one. So I used my then 250 connections from the UK to reach out to people they knew in Singapore. These people then said yes to meeting me, and from these chance encounters I got my first job which led to my second and my third.

My roles were marketing roles across the whole of Asia Pacific from China to Australia, Hong Kong to Indonesia, Thailand to India. I didn't know anyone in any of these countries, so I started using LinkedIn to reach out to people there, CEOs and CMOs, and they responded.

I was doing social selling before LinkedIn even coined the phrase. I was doing social selling when Sales Navigator hadn't even been thought of.

I merely used the data. I thought, "If I can find people for jobs in these countries, I can also find them to pitch them." Sure enough I could.

I was using what was a recruitment platform for social selling. I was using the data. That's why I know it works—I have won clients for multiple agencies doing this.

All this was being done authentically.

I then created Black Marketing because people kept asking me to train their teams in LinkedIn marketing and social selling. Then people started asking me to manage their profiles once I started winning the Official LinkedIn Power Profile awards.

I saw that no one else was doing LinkedIn for personal branding and social selling, and I understood that it didn't start and finish with recruitment, but that you could use this data in a different way. Thus, Black Marketing and my other brands started in this organic and authentic way.

Authenticity is key to success on LinkedIn.

I am the only LinkedIn trainer, masterclass instructor, or LinkedIn entrepreneur to have actually won the Official LinkedIn Power Profile Award year after year. In fact, I've won it every year that it has been awarded. No one else can claim that. That is part of my authentic credentials.

Practice what you preach and put what preach into action. If it works for me, then it'll work for my clients and my readers.

Social Proof: The Most Profound Authenticity

To be authentic, you have to be yourself. Dressing in a way you're not comfortable with or saying that you can do something when you can't is not authentically selling on LinkedIn. You will be found out, just like you would be in real life.

Just like in real life social situations and in B2C situations, in B2B on LinkedIn, it's all about being authentic. Whateverpast job experience, qualifications, and successful deliveries for previous clients that you list on your LinkedIn profile—it all must be true. When you share, "I did this", then you need social proof.

Social proof typically comes in the form of recommendations, which is why at Black Marketing we talk all the time about recommendations. We say, "Look at our 650 recommendations". Trust me, that's very powerful and convincing of Black Marketing's authenticity in delivering the success we promise.

Why? Because through our recommendations, it's not just me saying, "We know what we're doing when it comes to LinkedIn, LinkedIn masterclasses, personal branding, social selling and content marketing". When you provide recommendations, then it's actually other people saying how well you deliver in all these aspects too.

Here's a great example of recommendations as the most effective way of demonstrating your authenticity: people buy my masterclasses before they've even met me. Before they even contact me. When they do contact me, they don't ask, "Do you do LinkedIn masterclasses? Do you do personal branding masterclasses? How good are you? What evidence have you got that you're any good at this?" No, they never ask those questions.

When they contact me, they've already made up their minds—which is classic social selling. When they contact me, they say, "I looked at your LinkedIn profile, I've looked at your masterclasses on LinkedIn, I've looked at your masterclasses on YouTube, I've looked at all the people recommending you who've gone to your masterclasses. I've seen the pictures of you in action at your masterclasses. I've seen what people say about your masterclasses. I would like you to come and do a masterclass for me and for my company".

After that, it's just a matter of price and timing.

Again, this is classic social selling. They're coming to me because I'm sharing 650 people who recommend my services and also because I'm sharing content. They know I'm the real deal with 650 different people and businesses vouching for me.

Also, because I offer all my masterclasses on YouTube, they can view it for themselves and experience that content through a video and determine its high authenticity in that way. Because my content is authentically valuable, it also influences them to organise a masterclass with me.

Content Sharing: Another Avenue of Authenticity

Just as recommendations from your previous clients validate you, freely and openly sharing what you offer—and not keeping it secret—validates you in others' eyes as well. Of course, not every product or service is able to do this.

For instance, at Black Marketing, we have it established with our clients that we will never share the before-and-after nature of the work we do for them on their social media platforms. But, what I can openly share is the masterclass talks I give.

You might think that because I give out the videos of the masterclasses I do about LinkedIn and personal branding, it would count against me. No one would want to hire me to lead those classes at their organisations because they could just show the videos. In fact, the opposite is true. Those videos serve as convincing evidence—they add to my authenticity. They lead people to engage me.

My masterclasses are on the same subjects, but each time I deliver a masterclass, it ends up different. Why? Because my audience is different every single time. The energy I get is different every single time. The questions I get are different every single time. This is another reason why I don't lose anything by sharing videos of my masterclasses.

Here's another great example of how sharing your content adds to your authenticity and entices others to engage with you. My friend Fredrik Haren is one of the world's best global speakers on creativity and innovation. He's been to nearly seventy countries delivering presentations.

He explained to me that 95% of the people who hire him to speak do so after they hear him deliver a presentation in real life. Just think, he's hired to deliver a presentation to an audience, and as he's delivering the presentation, people in the audience are thinking to themselves, "Wow, this is amazing. I must employ him". That's the ultimate social selling. The other 5% come through people who view his videos on YouTube.

Fredrik is quite happy to give away his entire masterclass on YouTube because he knows by doing that viewers looking to hire speakers on creativity and innovation will be convinced of his authenticity and decide, "Wow, I need this guy".

No, the viewers don't think they can basically recreate his talk and show the YouTube video at a particular conference. Obviously, that does not work. You need real people in real life.

Because social selling involves person-to-person engagement, just as in real-life social situations, the most interesting and impressive engagement comes from authentic people. You must be authentic in your LinkedIn profile, in your personal branding, in your content marketing, and in your engagement with others for the social selling to succeed.

Two powerful ways to establish your authenticity are by offering social proof through people recommending you and by freely and openly offering renditions of your work, so people can experience it firsthand and determine your authenticity for themselves. When your authenticity is real and evident, you'll be rewarded with social selling success.

Along with authenticity, another critical component to social selling is personalisation. That's what we'll look at in the next chapter.

Chapter 18

Personalisation: Another Critical Component

Just as authenticity is critical in successful social selling, so is personalisation. When you connect with someone in real life at a conference, meeting, or over a cup of coffee, your engagement with them is personal. Similarly, when you connect with somebody over LinkedIn, do not spam them; do not send them a generic intro message; actually, personalise your message to them.

It makes the difference from them blowing off your message as an annoying sales pitch to them paying attention and wanting to at least respond to you because they can see that you know them and empathise with them.

How to Get Personal

Here's an example of a personalised approach that we at Black Marketing have used. For example, a CEO at a business pointed out to us the LinkedIn profile of one of their CEO friends at another business, confiding, "Chris, you all have done such amazing work helping us with our branding and turning our LinkedIn presence from pointless to powerful—I really wish you could work with Camille, my CEO friend at this business."

After examining Camille's LinkedIn page, both her own and that of her innovation company, my team wrote her a personalised message, beginning by telling her how it is she came to our attention from the CEO friend we both have in common. Next, we gave her precise changes she could make on her LinkedIn that would tremendously grow her presence, reach, and ultimately her bottom line.

Notice that our message was personal with Camille on a few levels. Number one: we drew her attention to a first connection we both shared. Number two: we drew her attention to some specific changes her LinkedIn could benefit from. From this personalised message Camille immediately saw us as empathetic, informed, interested, and known (via our shared first connection). She was willing to engage with us and explore the possibility of our working together. Getting personal has this potent effect in the social media and social selling space.

There are many options for personalising your contact with someone. For example, if you both worked at Google, you could say, "Oh, we're both Google alumni". If you went to the same university, you could point that out. When I lecture at universities in Hong Kong and Singapore, I emphasise the alumni network. I recommend, "Connect with other people from your university, both past and present, and actually say to them, 'We are both alumni of Singapore Management University', for example. 'Let's connect'".

When you personalise a message to someone and say something along the lines of, "We went to the same university, and I noticed you're the CMO of Google. I wonder if you could help me with how I could potentially get into Google. Would you be open to a having a coffee with me?" people will say yes because you used the alumni network. You're personalising your request, and that carries weight with people.

There are so many shared points of reference you can look for to refer to. Maybe you both are members of the same chamber of commerce. Maybe you both lived in London. Maybe you both studied marketing. Maybe you both know the same people. The point is to personalise your message.

I had someone say the other day, "Oh, we both have the same client". Fantastic. Somebody else said, "We both know this particular person, she's recommended to you". Or "We went to the same talk together", or "I read your content and I shared your post. I really liked it, and I'd love to talk to you".

As explained already in its own chapter, Sales Navigator is a great tool to employ to do very refined, filtered searches. You can use it to identify shared points of reference for others as well. From schooling to interests to previous workplaces and job positions—Sales Navigator can help you find relevant matches.

Also, Sales Navigator allows you to save leads, which offers future avenues for personal communications with these leads. You can save a lead and see what your lead is sharing, and if you like that lead's share, they will actually get a notification, saying, "Chris has liked my post", or "Chris has shared my post", or "Chris has commented on your post". That's personalisation.

When you save leads on Sales Navigator, you'll get notifications of their doings that you can then message them about. For example, I believe in congratulating people, so when I get a notification on LinkedIn saying, "This person's got a work anniversary", or "This person has changed jobs", I congratulate them.

I personalise my message by saying, "Congratulations on your new job. Let's talk together sometime about how Black Marketing can help you with your personal branding". Yes, I might be sending a sales-focused message, but I congratulate them first and then suggest, "Let's talk about your role as a new leader. You need to enhance your LinkedIn profile". Or "I noticed you haven't changed your profile", for example.

'Thank You' as Personalization

I can't recommend it enough that you answer every single blog post comment or share, thanking the person for doing so. I argue that even these quick, simple thank-yous are examples of personalisation.

You are taking the time to single out the individual who noticed and engaged with your content and you are offering a thanks. When you bother to do this, you'll find these people become very open and receptive to you, which increases your reach, social value, and, ultimately, your social sales.

It only makes sense that personalisation is so effective when it comes to social selling. Social selling is about relationships, engagement, person-to-person stuff. So the more we can show someone else that we know and care about them, in particular, the more appealing we are.

Social media platforms like Facebook, Instagram, or even WeChat, for example, don't offer relevant data about users. So much is unknown— their jobs, positions, ages, connections, etc. And really, because those aren't business community-oriented platforms and instead are family-, friend-, and entertainment-oriented, then that's fine.

To connect, build, and grow strong business relationships, we have LinkedIn. And LinkedIn gives us the data to connect and get appropriately personal—in the business context—so that our social selling can abound.

The next chapter revisits a crucial element to social selling that I've talked about some: the potent effect of reviews and recommendations. As you'll soon learn, when potential clients and buyers can read others' reviews of your work and get in touch with your past clients and buyers to talk about what it was like working with you, this increases their trust in you and willingness to take the plunge and work with you.

Chapter 19

Recommendations: Proof in the Social Selling Pudding

In the chapter on authenticity, I went into detail about how social proof in the form of people recommending you is indispensable for your social selling to take off. Because it's just that important, it's just that weighty, essential, and super powerful, I'm dedicating a single chapter to the super strength of recommendations in mastering social selling.

In any business, it is crucial that you get current and past clients (or buyers) to vouch for you, especially if you're in a personal business. If you're financial services or you're product ties, you sell the same stuff as many other places.

What's the difference? The difference is you. *You* are the differentiating factor that makes your business stellar. So, it's absolutely key that you stand out using your thought leadership, comments, personal branding, and recommendations.

Why should I choose you as my independent financial adviser as opposed to somebody else? Why should I choose you as my marketing agency as opposed to somebody else?

It's not just about awards because awards can be gamified. It's about recommendations. Real recommendations cannot be gamified. Genuine people who've been your genuine customers and who are recommending you in a genuine way.

On top of that, it's essential that these recommenders can be followed up on LinkedIn. Recommendations—real ones from clients and buyers who can be contacted on LinkedIn—that's going to give you the social proof you need for your social selling to move from an exchange of messages to a real discussion about working together, which means making sales.

Confidentiality Issues?

Perhaps your business is like mine, Black Marketing, and you have people frequently asking you for case studies. Perhaps, like Black Marketing, you have confidentiality agreements or other special contracts with clients, so you simply can't show any before-and-after examples to potential clients or buyers.

Because we at Black Marketing assist other businesses, CEOs, and entrepreneurs in revamping their LinkedIn profiles, creating compelling employer branding campaigns and social selling campaigns and developing razor-sharp personal branding, there are many instances when it is people on my teams at Black Marketing who are writing blogs, writing comments, and engaging with people in the name of CEOs and other decision-makers at big businesses.

For this reason, we have confidentiality agreements with the businesses we work with. We don't want them to have any worry of getting called out for the writing and engagement help we provide them. Also, in our agreements, any writing we do for a client becomes writing that the client owns. This means we can't refer to it. It's not ours to show to leads asking for examples of our work.

It is in this context that it is even more remarkable that I have 650 LinkedIn recommendations, the most of anyone doing what I do: LinkedIn talks, LinkedIn marketing, social selling for clients, and personal branding clients. Many clients simply won't recommend us because by doing so they are admitting that Black Marketing has been managing their profiles. So to get 650 people to give us recommendations is amazing. Like McKinsey, we don't talk about our clients, but some of our clients talk about us.

What do I do when potential clients ask to see case studies of Black Marketing work? I supply the names and companies that recommend us on LinkedIn and PointDrive.

I encourage all my clients and the people who attend my masterclasses to give me recommendations on LinkedIn. Part of these recommendations is their willingness to be contacted by people interested in working with me.

Then, I ask people interested in hiring me to contact any and all of these people who have recommended me. I say, "Please feel free to click through to those people who recommend us and actually ask them what it was like to deal with Black Marketing. What was it like to work with The Dark Art of Marketing? What was it like to participate in one of Chris's masterclasses?" I urge both parties to discuss me and my business frankly because authenticity is essential when it comes to recommendations.

Whether you have confidentiality agreements or other stipulations, you must find a way to get recommendations. Others vouching for you and your business, especially when these people can be privately messaged over LinkedIn without you as the medium, gives you the needed authority for prospects to get serious about working you. It amps up your social selling.

Recommendations take your engagement with others from comments, shares, likes, and quick messages to serious enquiries on how to collaborate together—that means sales.

In the next chapter, we explore another convincing means of social proof: your bestselling book. I'm going to let you in on how it's much less stressful to write, publish, and market your own book than you might think. Plus, a book makes a memorable business card!

Chapter 20

The Ultimate: Your Bestselling Book

We've already discussed how important establishing your social proof is to your success at social selling. We talked about the powerful social proof you gain when you can give evidence of the many people and businesses that recommend you.

In this chapter, we'll discuss another potent form of social proof—your #1 bestselling book. Writing a book, particularly one that becomes a bestseller in its field, gives you tremendous social proof on many different levels, all of which will result in you enjoying successful social selling. Surprisingly, it isn't as laborious to write a book as you might think!

Credibility, Personal Branding, and Value

When you write a book, sharing your experiences and lessons learnt in your particular area of expertise, then this book touches on—and adds to—all those components needed for your social selling to take off. From the content you impart and from the fact you had the foresight to organise it, shape it, and publish it in a book, you further establish your authority and credibility, both of which are significant elements to social selling.

Earlier in this book, when we talked about personal branding, I explained that central to personal branding lies your values, style, thought leadership, and platform. In writing a book, you are able to literally write out, explicitly, for all to read, your exact values and then repeatedly you can give examples in the book that show you enacting those values. In this way, you put yourself in charge of your personal brand.

By writing a book, you, yourself, are the one cultivating your personal brand's narrative, as opposed to just hoping for the best and letting people discover whatever they can in their own social research.

Your style is also a big component of personal branding. For me, my authentic style comes across visually in the Mohawk I sport and my black rock t-shirts, black ripped jeans, and Doc Martens because that's me at my most comfortable and creative. Your book is another avenue for you to relay your authentic style. Your personal branding.

You'll notice that the voice, phrasing, and word choices in my book, the one that you are reading now, reflect my over-the-top passion for what I do as well as my brainy punk-rocker style. That's what your book can do for you too—promote your authentic style—which is a huge component of personal branding and of successful social selling.

Thought leadership, both in personal branding and in social selling, is paramount. When you write a book, giving in detail your experiences, lessons learnt, and big ideas in your area of expertise, the book is literally a testament to your thought leadership. Nothing is more powerful than that. Think about it in terms of me and my book, the very one you are reading (which is actually my third book!).

In this book I'm teaching you about social selling, sharing all I've learnt from my own personal experiences and from my business's work guiding clients. At the same time that this book imparts valuable information that you can put to use to increase your social selling, over and over again, on another level this book imparts too that I am an expert in my field.

It shows me as a thought leader. "Chris really knows what he's talking about", your mind might be thinking on some level as you read this book. This is exactly what your readers will be thinking when they read your book—and it's what you want because it's what will lead to them contacting you or recommending you to others they know.

In this way, you establish yourself as an expert and thought leader in your field. Also you further cement your personal brand. When you publish a book, then you won't have to convince people that you are an expert, that you are credible—they'll already know it when they come to you because they've learnt all about you, your background, and accomplishments in your book.

Remember—in today's world of social media, people are doing a lot of research about services, products, and the people behind them before they buy, so when they come to you, they've already made their decision.

Your book puts you in the driver's seat in terms of the research they do about you. They will read all that you, yourself, have crafted to help them decide what they think of you!

The final part of personal branding and social selling is deciding on your primary platform. As you certainly know by now, I'm a beyond-one-hundred-percent LinkedIn guy. To add icing on that cake, I've also written three books. L inkedIn and my books make up my platform and promote my personal brand, my expertise, my leadership, my business, my social selling, and, of course, my content marketing. These platforms perfectly complement one another too.

When I meet people at conferences, events, or even at the airport, our conversations may result in me giving them one of my books (talk about an unforgettable "business card" of sorts!). Next, when they read it, it leads them to engage with me on LinkedIn.

From there they may decide they want to work with Black Marketing. Or, it might happen in the other direction—I connect with them via LinkedIn (or they connect with me); then we meet in real life at a conference, masterclass, or for a coffee, and I give them one of my books. A fter reading my book, they are then convinced that they want to work with me and Black Marketing. When you add a book to your primary platform, it adds a supercharge to your social selling machine, getting it running at an even higher speed.

What are your platforms? Do they work well together to lead and convince people to engage with you and even employ you (or buy your products)? A book will complement your main platform and lead more people to you.

Marketing, Not Money

It's very important to be sure of your objectives when writing a book. You are not writing it to make money directly from book sales. Why? Because you write it to position yourself as an expert in your field. Then you give your book out to everyone, so that when they read it, they are helped out by your content and at the same time they draw the conclusion that, indeed, you are an expert.

Share your content—your book—and then share it again and again. Instead of a business card, I give out my books to people when I meet them. I give out books at my talks and masterclasses. My books are everywhere. Yes, they are also available on Amazon, globally, in every format—from Kindle to audiobook, from hardback to paperback. However, I do that all very cost effectively to get my content and expertise out there and to market Black Marketing's services as well. This is what you should do with your book to make it work in your social selling grand plan.

Remember—a huge component of social selling rests on you giving away content that helps to position you as a leader in your field.

About Your Writing Dread . . .

Writing a book has never been easier, especially for super busy business people who don't consider themselves so-called "professional" writers. Realise that you aren't looking to win a Nobel Prize in Literature with your book—and for that matter, your readers aren't looking to read something highfalutin and overly crafted either.

In your book, they want your genuine voice, stories, and thoughts, stuff they can immediately grasp and put to use. This doesn't take a genius to do, but it does take persistence and organising. The great thing is when you write a book nowadays, you don't even have to write it.

"What? What do you mean, Chris?" I hear you questioning in utter disbelief.

Here's what I mean: you can talk your book out and record it all on your smart device. Next, you can get a company to make written transcripts of your words.

Lots of companies offer services like this at very reasonable rates. After this, by yourself or with a professional editor, you can shape those transcripts into book form. Then you can market it through your existing marketing channels and self-publish it.

Evolve to the Rescue!

Even better, you can work with a company that will help you organise all these steps. I've worked with Evolve Global Publishing (www. evolveglobalpublishing.com) for the books I've written, including this one. Yes, I highly recommend them!

Evolve Global Publishing offers various packages, so whether you're a novice or you have experience, they've got something for you. For more information, visit www.evolveglobalpublishing.com. Whatever you pay Evolve Global Publishing, you should see it as an investment because the doors the resulting book will open for you are many, and those many doors will lead to increased social sales.

Because your personal brand, your expertise, your clientele, and your business are constantly developing and growing, it means that your means of social selling—whether that be your content marketing strategy, LinkedIn profile, or your Sales Navigator searches—should never be static.

To stay on point, you've got to be regularly testing and changing. That's what we'll discuss in the next chapter.

Chapter 21

Test, Test, Test, Change, Change, Change, Iterate, Iterate, Iterate

As individuals, we are constantly developing and growing and changing. Our businesses are the same. As we take on new projects or products, our expertise deepens or grows in another capacity. In this way our stories change too—who we are, what we've done, what we can do, and what we want to do—it's always changing. As we work with more and more clients and buyers, not only do our skills grow but the number of people recommending our services grows. Also, the areas of our service that they are recommending grow and change.

These are reasons that you can't expect the LinkedIn profile you make on day one or your first successful content marketing strategy to stay that way for years and continue working really well. As you and your business grow, develop, and change—as well as your prospective clients' businesses—your profile and your means of social selling must change too.

Plus, the capacities and offerings of our chosen social media platforms change. To stay relevant and vibrant on the platform, we have to change and put to use their new offerings. Since I started using LinkedIn, what it offers me has changed a lot over the years— videos, PointDrive, Sales Navigator. Even the search options on Sales Navigator have changed. Additionally, there are new businesses and business people signing up to LinkedIn all the time, so these are new connections for me to make, engage with, and cultivate. My first, second, and third connections are changing.

This regular change means that we, in turn, can never land on a single, established method for social selling. Instead, we must constantly be responding to change—testing, changing, and iterating as well.

Changes in Content Marketing

If you're no longer getting sufficient engagement, change your content marketing strategy. Change your content itself! Change your short posts or long posts. Don't do graphs, don't do long form, don't do white papers, and do something else instead. Do something more accessible. Do more videos.

People only have a few minutes to look at content. So if you went from getting lots of engagement to little, check out your content marketing strategy and change it. Test, change, and iterate until you can get more engagement again.

Perhaps you need to add more connections in a particular area? Do more content, do more social selling, do more videos? Change the data, change who you're targeting. Change so you're targeting active people on LinkedIn, not just anybody. Notice too how your second and third connections are growing and changing—this affects the success of your content marketing and social selling.

No one and nothing is static. To stay in the game and at the top, you must be regularly changing.

Changes to Sales Navigator

Because of all the other changes happening within the LinkedIn platform itself or with its users, what you can find is that how you use Sales Navigator, after a time, may no longer be effective. So, you need to change that too. Test change, and iterate.

You may need to change your headline, change your body copy, change your parameters, change your data, change who you're targeting. You may need to see if those you are targeting are still active on LinkedIn. LinkedIn allows you to do it.

LinkedIn's a fantastic platform. It's a very creative platform. It allows you lots of different ways to target lots of different people. And that's the same thing with messaging. If your messaging is not working and Sales Navigator's not working, change your targeting. Change it to people who actually change jobs or people who are in the news or people who are active on LinkedIn.

About headline changes—one of my best headlines actually says, "I'm visiting your city. I'd love to come and talk to you. I'm only available for five days. Let's talk about your LinkedIn marketing [or your personal branding]".

The point is that you can make changes and test them to see how they work. Change your headline and then ask, "Okay, what results did that have? How do I actually get more results as a result of it?"

Test, test, test. Change, change, change. Iterate, iterate, iterate.

LinkedIn allows you to do it: change everything and take note of the results. Because social media is social and rests on people and relationships—we know how those are always changing—some grow more robust; others fizzle. To stay relevant and keep your social selling vibrant, test, change, and iterate your strategies.

To wrap up this book, in our final chapters we'll explore how you and I might collaborate to get your social selling in top form. The final chapters are all about Black Marketing and all we can offer you and what our clients say about us.

Chapter 22

More on Black Marketing: The Most Recommended Social Selling Agency on LinkedIn

Your LinkedIn personal profile never sleeps. Google yourself or your company, and your LinkedIn profile comes up top. What impression does it give to potential clients, investors, employees, media, and partners?

When you team up with Black Marketing, you have ensured a LinkedIn personal profile that you will be proud of and that enables you to achieve all of your business objectives. Personal branding, company branding, new business, finding clients, reaching out, and thought leadership—all of these goals can be achieved on LinkedIn, and Black Marketing can give you that leg up.

We at Black Marketing are the experts on LinkedIn.

We know what we are doing on LinkedIn, and we spend a lot of time on LinkedIn finding out what to do and what not to do. We know how to game the system so that we can benefit our clients.

That's why people use Black Marketing.

A Profile of Black Marketing Clients

Black Marketing's clients tends to be CEOs, founders, MDs in charge of their own businesses, regional MDs heading global businesses, and entrepreneurs. Our clients simply don't have the time themselves to maximise their LinkedIn profiles, plan their content marketing on

LinkedIn, create new business on LinkedIn, and manage/develop their company pages on LinkedIn. They are prepared to outsource it to us because it makes good commercial and business sense to do so.

DIY or Outsource to Experts?

Many people choose not to outsource and either do it themselves or get someone internally to do the job for them. Is this the best avenue to take for their business to thrive?

There is no wrong and right answer here; everyone is different. Nevertheless, the question remains—

If you keep the service in-house or do it yourself, will you get the same level of experience of making the most of LinkedIn? Will you get the same quality service and the same high level of expertise that Black Marketing gives? Will you get the same results? Only you can decide what's best for you.

Many people try to do this themselves. They soon discover that they can't find the time to dedicate to it every day and week. Accordingly, they don't have the time to make the most of all of the great commercial and marketing potential of LinkedIn, like getting their LinkedIn blog on LinkedIn's Pulse. Alternatively, they realise that they are not using all of LinkedIn's many different facets; therefore, they are not maximising their LinkedIn presence.

The New Little Black Book

Gone are the days when recruiters check your Facebook profile to scan your photos in hope of dissecting your personality. They will, though, check who knows you on LinkedIn. This is where those two or three degrees of separation kick in again. The same applies in business for clients.

The easiest thing in the world for a client to check is which mutual people you know and, in turn, to ask them what they think of you, what your company was like to work with, and whether you delivered.

LinkedIn is your new "little black book"; don't forget it and keep growing it.

You never know where opportunities may lie, whatever your business objective. Remember, "It's not what you know, it's *who* you know."

Black Marketing is the world's most recommended LinkedIn marketing agency, created and led by the world's most recommended LinkedIn marketing masterclass instructor, entrepreneur, founder with 650 LinkedIn recommendations, triple LinkedIn marketing bestselling author, and the only one who is an official LinkedIn Power Profile seven years running—Chris J. Reed.

Chris's Black Marketing is an award-winning, independent, boutique B2B marketing consultancy that specialises in enabling you to achieve your business objectives through LinkedIn. Chris and his team provide the following LinkedIn marketing services:

- Your personal LinkedIn profile, managed and developed
- Your personal brand accentuated on LinkedIn
- Your company LinkedIn profile, managed and developed
- Your employer brand elevated through LinkedIn
- Your content marketing strategy, created and implemented for you on LinkedIn

From our collaboration together, we'll provide you with significant support, so you can:

- Win new business through LinkedIn
- Create and implement social selling strategies on LinkedIn
- Use Sales Navigator to generate leads
- Become a thought leader on LinkedIn
- Increase your search rankings on both LinkedIn and Google
- Train your team on LinkedIn best practises

For more information, please visit Black Marketing's LinkedIn company page, Black Marketing, or their website: https://www.blackmarketing.com

Four Additional Brands

Chris actually has four other brands that also use LinkedIn in various ways to market individuals. Here are those four additional brands:

(1) The Dark Art of Marketing—Personal Branding Mastery for Entrepreneurs—Personal PR for You

Welcome to The Dark Art of Marketing—Personal Branding for Entrepreneurs—Personal PR for You The Dark Art of Marketing will transform your personal brand to rock-star status on and beyond LinkedIn. We essentially manage and develop your personal PR strategy.

Your personal brand is the key to your future success.

Invest in it now.

- If you are leader/CEO, this is essential for you
- If you are an entrepreneur wanting clients, funding, employees, media coverage or you want a higher profile, a greater thought leadership status, and a more tangible all-round personal brand, this is for you.
- If you are a non-executive director looking for more positions, this is for you.
- If you are an author or want to be an author, this is for you.
- If you are a speaker or want to be a speaker, this is for you.
- If you want to be a thought leader, this is for you.
- If you just want to build up your personal brand because you know how important it is for you now and in the future, this is for you.

Led by multi-award-winning LinkedIn Power Profile, entrepreneur, CEO, founder, three-time #1 international bestselling author, most recommended LinkedIn entrepreneur with 650 LinkedIn recommendations and serial entrepreneur, Chris J Reed, The Dark Art of Marketing manages all aspects of your personal brand/PR campaign:

- Thought leadership in all places possible from business media to your industry media and LinkedIn (we write all the articles for you or use yours)
- Getting you speaking engagements for both PR and paid-for events
- Creating and managing your YouTube channel for you
- Entering awards for you
- Trading PR for you
- Enabling you to become a bestselling author
- Using LinkedIn to amplify and perform the catalyst role for all of the above

(2) Mohawk Marketing—TripAdvisor Engagement for You

For those of you who own venues specifically for business people to use, whether it's a leisure venue, hotel, villa, bar, restaurant, cafe, MICE space, or any other space, we now have a service for you too. Mohawk Marketing combines TripAdvisor with LinkedIn to ensure that you are maximising your B2B marketing and revenue generation.

If you are not managing your own TripAdvisor pages, we can do that for you. If you are but wish to outsource it, we can do that for you too.

Our USP is that we then share these reviews on LinkedIn and engage through LinkedIn's Sales Navigator to find new clients for you. We engage your customers for you.

We service entrepreneurs in the travel, hospitality, leisure, and tourism space as well as multinational chains of hotels, restaurants, and leisure and tourist attractions.

We manage your TripAdvisor page for you so that you don't need to. Then we use LinkedIn to amplify the positive reviews and use your profile to target the 650 million business travellers on LinkedIn that could be your customers.

TripAdvisor is the largest travel site in the world with 315 million active members. You need to engage them to ensure that your brand stands out and is recommended to others as well as encourages brand loyalty and repeat visits.

TripAdvisor drives the majority of your customers to your venue whether you like it or not. Therefore, you must be actively engaging all customers on TripAdvisor. We can do that for you. We can help you save time and help you turn bad and average reviews into your best advocates and help you to capitalise on your positive reviews.

We will take over and manage your TripAdvisor page or pages for you.

Services:

- We help you create your TripAdvisor page if it's not already set up.
- We upgrade you to the premium level.
- We upgrade your rankings on TripAdvisor.
- We work with you on the media, creativity, and videos that can be used to better drive engagement and sales on your TripAdvisor page.
- We manage all of your replies to all reviews, positive, average, and negative, for you.
- We agree on ways to communicate effectively to everyone who comments on your page on TripAdvisor.
- We help you analyse all the data on your TripAdvisor page and make recommendations to you.
- We work with you on running offers and driving bookings.
- Essentially we do everything on TripAdvisor for you.

When we work with you, either managing your TripAdvisor page or using your great TripAdvisor reviews, we start by marketing your venue on LinkedIn to 650 million affluent professionals. These are professionals looking to book your venue for corporate hospitality, corporate accommodation, or corporate private dining for team building and/or client nights. We help you market your venue to the business community in your country and region through your profile and your company page on LinkedIn.

(3) Chris J Reed Mastery—Masterclasses that Engage, Educate, Delight, and Entertain

My LinkedIn masterclass is for you if you wish to inspire your leadership team, C-suite, marketing and sales teams, and employees.

I am also the only LinkedIn Power Profile Winner seven years running who is offering LinkedIn masterclasses, and I will show you how you can transform your LinkedIn profiles to achieve all of your objectives in a professional context and enable your company to achieve its objectives too.

What you get from my LinkedIn Masterclass:

- Your team will be trained on all aspects of LinkedIn relevant for their roles.
- Your team will be shown LinkedIn best practises, getting the most out of the LinkedIn platform.
- Every part of LinkedIn can be demonstrated, enabling your team full practical use straight after the session.
- We customise and personalise the masterclass to your requests and needs.
- We also go through every single person's profile in the masterclass, demonstrating what they should and should not be doing in a very engaging and interactive way.

You may also check out my 650 recommendations that I have received about my acclaimed LinkedIn masterclasses, workshops, talks, and what Black Marketing has done for clients. Feel free to contact anyone on this list and ask them directly how engaging, interactive, inspirational, and educational my sessions are.

I wrote the #1 international bestselling books about LinkedIn, personal branding, and social selling, and I will share my experience and knowledge on every detail of how to use LinkedIn, specifically covering what to do and what not to do across the four main pillars of LinkedIn success: personal branding, employer/company branding, content marketing/thought leader elevation, and Sales Navigator, social selling, and messaging.

(4) Spark: LinkedIn + Tinder = Match

Spark combines Tinder with LinkedIn to help professionals on LinkedIn find love with other people on LinkedIn who are also looking for a relationship.

Spark manages professionals' Tinder profiles to ensure that they present the best possible version of themselves. We then add the LinkedIn element to this by ensuring that the professional's LinkedIn profile is at rock-star level and then we share these details on Tinder.

While we are managing the Tinder profiles for professionals, we are ensuring that they are only matched with similar professionals who also have genuine LinkedIn profiles.

By combining both brands we overcome key concerns on both platforms:

Concern 1) *That a Tinder profile is fake*
Now that you can link your LinkedIn profile to your Tinder profile, professionals on Tinder can check out your professional profile to make sure that you are a real person with a real career/job. This provides a more substantial platform for a longer lasting relationship, should you be looking for this with a like-minded professional. Spark ensures this by linking the Tinder and LinkedIn profiles together.

Concern 2) *That women on LinkedIn feel that they are targeted through their photos for romantic relationships*
Now women can deflect this away and say "If I were looking, I would be on Tinder, and then you could see my LinkedIn profile there.

If this is not the case, you have no basis to contact me on LinkedIn for a romantic relationship." Spark ensures this by linking the Tinder and LinkedIn profiles together.

Concern 3) *Many people meet their romantic partners through a work situation*

Whether this is in the same office, same company but in different countries, through a client/agency relationship, at an event, or through a referral, no one can deny that work creates the basis for many romantic relationships. But how do you ensure that the person that you are romantically interested in is also looking for someone? Spark ensures this by linking the Tinder and LinkedIn profiles together.

Spark: LinkedIn + Tinder = Match

Chapter 23
What People Are Saying about Black Marketing and Chris J. Reed

Thank you, Chris! Brilliant main stage keynote presentation on LinkedIn marketing and personal branding at the ACTE Global Summit Singapore. It was an insightful, interactive session filled with relevant examples and content.

John Holden
Executive Coach at Mind Odyssey
Regional BD Director at Mercuri International
Special Consultant at ACTE Global

Chris is an inspiring leader who led the company to a greater height. I had the pleasure of working with him during my time with Black Marketing. I was particularly impressed by Chris's ability to command a room and get people on board with ideas—even people who were initially on completely different pages. Not only that, I respect his dedication and passion towards Black Marketing. No matter how tense a meeting, Chris always makes sure everyone left with a smile. I dare to say, Black Marketing does the best LinkedIn marketing.

Samantha Lee Wealth Accumulation
Consultant Marketing Manager
Social Selling 2018

Chris gave a highly-charged presentation that certainly impacted the atmosphere of the ACTE Global Summit. His examples of how successful leaders have built a strong following on LinkedIn were enlightening.

Esther Lew
Editor-in-Chief
Northstar Travel Media

I enjoyed Chris's speech very much at ACTE opening ceremony. He is very fun and energetic, great engagement with the audience! His talk is very inspiring, and I highly recommend him and his book to any professionals and companies as it will definitely help you build your unique personal brand!

Anja Jia
APAC Business Relationship Manager
ATG (AllStars Travel Group)

Chris's presentation for AmCham HK was one of the most upbeat, engaging, and useful hours I've spent in a workshop. Great speaker.

Diana Wu David
Founder
Sarana Capital / Sarana Labs

MAs, the old cliche goes, "Don't judge a book by its cover". In this case, it was spot-on with Chris; I had no idea what to expect and wondered what this keynote speaker with a Mohawk was going to offer me. Within moments of his arrival on stage, it became electrifying, eye-opening, and some would say mind-blowing.

Chris is hands-down the best speaker I have had the pleasure to listen to and experience up close because he was able to push the right buttons while sharing his world through his unique lens. Chris is the poster child for a high-energy, personable speaker who brings the conversation to life, almost 3-D.

If you want to up your game with your next meeting, he's the one you want to coach you and your team on branding, interpersonal skills,

120

presentations, and how to approach life with zest and fervour. Twenty-four hours later, we're still all talking about his presentation and how it positively impacted us.

Steve Sitto
Global Travel & Meetings Manager
Tesla, Inc.

I was a facilitator at nEbO YES 2018 when I met Chris for the second time, and there I finally grew the courage to go up to him and network. The first time I met him was at nEbO YES 2017. On both occasions, Chris has been nothing but inspirational, driven, and very energetic. He became an instant idol and an influencer in my journey as an entrepreneur from then on. That's all I can say, he's the best at what he does. If you say personal branding, I say Chris J. Reed.

Kaung Htet Htun
President
NYP Entrepreneurship Club | Nursing Student

Chris presented an insightful and entertaining 'Top Tips on How to Use LinkedIn' workshop at HSBC. He is an engaging and knowledgeable speaker. I learnt a great deal from his workshop. Thank you.

Helen Siah
Senior Corporate Services and Event Manager
HSBC

Mohawk is awesome! He shares practical tips and techniques that everyone can do and follow to enhance their own personal branding. As a startup owner, I have to work everything on lean, and Mohawk has shown how things should work digitally as well as in real life. I'd definitely recommend any professionals to join his workshops and/or get his books.

Connie Tsui-Burchfield
Transforming Leaders, Businesses, and Communities
Through Empowerment

Chris's talk came at just the right time for me as I was making my first forays into LinkedIn publishing and posting. He's a great communicator and had some really useful practical tips, all backed up with memorable examples of how to get it right—and wrong!

Peter Williams
Former Managing Director
British Chamber of Commerce in China and China-Britain Business Council

Chris is one of the most original, connected, and dynamic people I know. He has transformed how individuals and businesses "use" LinkedIn, and his insights and value-add are legendary. An open, creative, informed, and a very funny guy, Chris will add value to your personal or business life as soon as he becomes part of your world. Invite him in! I believe you can find him on LinkedIn . . .

Charles Lankester
EVP
Global Reputation and Risk Management Practice

Chris volunteered to come down and speak to a group of budding entrepreneurs in the Youth Entrepreneurship Symposium 2018. He delivered a splendid talk on branding yourself on LinkedIn, which the participants loved. It was truly amazing to see him speak. I was not only entertained the entire way but also managed to take home some important lessons, which I immediately began to apply. All in all, Chris was a joy to liaise and work with, and I sincerely hope we meet again.

Ethan Wong
Murdoch University Student
Committee Member
Institute of Public Relations Singapore, Murdoch University Chapter

Chris delivered a fantastic speech for us this week in Hong Kong. He is a very likable character, and he knows how to keep an audience engaged. Aside from the tips around LinkedIn usage, which most people were not aware of, he has a natural skill to get you thinking about yourself—specifically how you come across to other people. I could see a lot of nodding heads in the audience. His masterclass show is thoroughly recommended in any context, be it business or just pure entertainment!

Steve Travis
Chief Administration Officer
HSBC Hong Kong

Chris was a concurrent keynote speaker at the Youth Entrepreneurship Symposium 2018. He shared his insights on personal branding and effective LinkedIn profiles with youths interested in entrepreneurship from the ages of 17 to 25. We received positive feedback from participants on his high level of engagement with them as well as on the helpfulness of his keynote session. He is also approachable and easygoing towards event organisers, which made working with him a breeze!

Imrenjeet Kaur
President
Youth Entrepreneurship Symposium 2018 at nEbO

Chris is profoundly passionate about his craft. He has a lot to offer anyone looking to market their core competency. But perhaps his greatest talent is the ability to listen, observe, and accept changing environments. This is how he prospers; his clients can't help but do the same.

Steve Dawson
Business Communication, Presentation, and Public Speaking Coach

Chris and his team are really experts in LinkedIn marketing strategies, creating large visibility for individuals and corporates.

Luiz Simione
CEO
Bradesco Securities—APAC | Corporate,
Institutional and Investment Banking | Asset
Management | Business Growth

Chris and his team have been such a huge help in my everyday work. They are definitely the go-to experts for enhancing your personal brand and LinkedIn marketing strategies. If you're looking to build your personal brand using LinkedIn, I recommend working with Chris.

Geraldine Critchley
Director of Marketing
@Nine.ch | Cloud Evangelist | Hybrid and Multi-
Cloud | B2B Marketing Strategist and Leader

Chapter 24
Chris's Other Books

Chris has written two other #1 international bestselling books on marketing. Check them out below to add to your library.

LinkedIn Mastery for Entrepreneurs

If you wish to achieve great things in the business world, LinkedIn is the first logical place to start the process of building your personal brand. *LinkedIn Mastery for Entrepreneurs* was written for anyone who wishes to maximise the many applications of LinkedIn to build their personal brand. By employing LinkedIn to achieve your objectives, you must learn to harness the process of becoming a thought leader on LinkedIn. This book teaches you all about it! If you would like to read more of Chris's 650 LinkedIn recommendations please visit his LinkedIn profile, Slide Share profile or his Point Drive decks

Get it on:
- **Amazon:** https://amzn.to/2vtzEgw
- **Chris's website:** http://www.chrisjreed.com/

Personal Branding for Entrepreneurs

In this book, Chris tells you all about how you, as an entrepreneur, can develop your personal brand beyond LinkedIn. You see, as an entrepreneur, your personal brand is what everyone is buying into. Your clients, shareholders, employees, partners, the media . . . your future clients, employees, investors—they are all buying into the power and values of your personal brand. That's why you need to start working on it now, which is exactly what Chris's *Personal Branding for Entrepreneurs* teaches you to do.

- **Amazon:** https://amzn.to/2M5gqbo
- **Chris's website:** http://www.chrisjreed.com/